HAPPY IS UP
SAD IS DOWN

HAPPY IS UP
SAD IS DOWN

65 metaphors for design

Jörn Hurtienne

Diana Löffler

Clara Hüsch

Daniel Reinhardt

Robert Tscharn

Stephan Huber

BIS Publishers
Building Het Sieraad
Postjesweg 1
1057 DT Amsterdam
The Netherlands
T +31 (0)20 515 02 30
bis@bispublishers.com
www.bispublishers.com

ISBN 978 90 6369 5934

Design & Illustrations: Clara Hüsch

Contents

About This Book 8

Metaphors
1. BASIC UNITS 19
2. BASIC JUDGEMENTS 61
3. EMOTIONS 111
4. SOCIAL RELATIONS 145
5. KNOWLEDGE & COMMUNICATION 191
6. ECONOMICS & POLITICS 225
7. ETHICS & TRANSCENDENCE 259

Authors 292
You Want More? 295
References 296
The Whole Book in One Picture INSIDE BACK COVER

Metaphor is not only a linguistic device.

We use metaphors to think and talk about one kind of thing in terms of another.[1] When we talk metaphorically, we often use words describing basic physical properties to express something more abstract: judgements, emotions and values. When goods become more expensive, for example, we say *prices are going up* – but the price tags stay in the same place. When someone is friendly on the first encounter, we say *they gave me a warm reception* – even if we met outside in the freezing cold. When we have an honest conversation with someone, we might say *thank you for being straight with me* – even though we are both slouching on the sofa. Metaphors are omnipresent: around 12% of our words are used metaphorically.[2] Most of these metaphors are dead; we do not realise that we are using them.

Metaphors are intuitive patterns of thought.

Besides being a figure of speech, metaphoric language offers a window into how we think. Many metaphoric expressions are the same across different languages. For example, the expression *straight talk* can be found in languages like English, Hungarian, Japanese and Russian.[3] Because many metaphoric expressions seem to be identical across languages, cognitive linguists have concluded that metaphors are not just a matter of language – they must also be a matter of thought.[4]

This book is about primary metaphors. They are called *primary* because they are derived from basic experiences and can be used as the basis for more complex metaphors. Primary metaphors are learned in our early years. They form when we repeatedly co-experience something physical with a more abstract evaluation.[5] The water level in a glass, for example, is related to the quantity of water in the glass (**MORE IS UP – LESS IS DOWN**). Cuddling up to loved ones we feel their body heat and experience comfort and friendliness at the same time (**FRIENDLY IS WARM**). Being honest is often connected with a straight body position and a direct gaze (**MORAL IS STRAIGHT**). Repeatedly experiencing the co-occurrence of specific physical experiences with abstract judgements strongly links these concepts in the brain. Later, these links can be automatically activated even when the original physical experience is absent. Thus, a welcome can still feel warm, even without body contact.

The idea that primary metaphors are implicit patterns of thought sparked much interest in psychology. Over the past 15 years, psychologists have been testing this idea in various studies. For example, when we ask people whether they associate a warm or a cold glass of water with the concept *friendly*, most people select the warm glass, reliving the primary metaphor **FRIENDLY IS WARM – UNFRIENDLY IS COLD.**[6]

In another study, people were first given either a hot or a cold drink as part of the introduction phase. Then their task was to answer some questions about another person, e.g. whether she had a friendly or unfriendly personality. Participants who held a hot drink rated the other person as being friendlier than those who held a cold drink.[7] Thus, the primary metaphor **FRIENDLY IS WARM – UNFRIENDLY IS COLD** was automatically triggered by feeling the temperature of the drink and it influenced what people thought.

Metaphors are intuitive patterns for design.

As metaphors point to the way we intuitively think, why not use them as design patterns to make our artefacts more viscerally appealing? Designers already implicitly apply primary metaphors: in data charts, cartoons, advertisements, architecture, products and their user interfaces. Look, for example, at a single-lever water tap. It is easy to operate: the higher you move the lever, the stronger the water flow. Look at volume sliders. We immediately know that to decrease the volume we need to move the slider down and to increase it we need to move it up. These mappings, going back to the primary metaphor **MORE IS UP – LESS IS DOWN,** are so intuitive that these controls do not even need a label. Other designs like spin boxes, thermometers and stock market graphs also implement this metaphor.

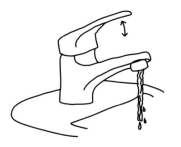
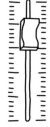

Using metaphors, abstract concepts can be conveyed with physical and spatial means. Although designers often implicitly employ primary metaphors, making these explicit allows for a greater range of creative possibilities. Applying primary metaphors in design has been demonstrated to come with three advantages. Metaphor-aligned designs are perceived as more innovative, intuitive to use and inclusive.[8]

More innovative, because metaphors reduce the mappings between the abstract and the physical to their essence and inspire playful and uncommon designs. More intuitive to use, because metaphors build on our basic world knowledge that we automatically apply. More inclusive, because this knowledge is shared by most people around the globe and of different abilities. To make these metaphors ready to hand, we have collected them in this book.

MORE IS UP
LESS IS DOWN

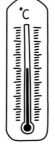
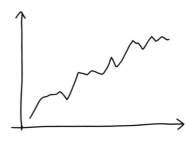

This book is for designers ...

and user experience researchers, marketers, human factors specialists, linguists, psychologists, philosophers – basically everyone interested in how the mind works and how to apply this knowledge to understand and change the world.

The book contains a collection of 65 primary metaphors to be used as inspiration for creating physical and digital artefacts that intuitively communicate abstract ideas by using physical and spatial means. To make the metaphors easy to find and readily applicable, we have clustered them into seven groups: Basic Units, Basic Judgements, Emotions, Social Relations, Knowledge & Communication, Economics & Politics, Ethics & Transcendence. A graphical overview at the end of the book shows which physical properties are connected to which abstract concepts.

In the main part of the book, each metaphor is introduced on two double pages. The metaphor names follow the structure **ABSTRACT TARGET DOMAIN IS PHYSICAL SOURCE DOMAIN** to show how the abstract and the physical are connected, e.g. **MORAL IS STRAIGHT – CORRUPT IS CROOKED.** Each initial double page (1) illustrates the metaphor and shows how it is expressed in three languages (English, German and Japanese).

(1)

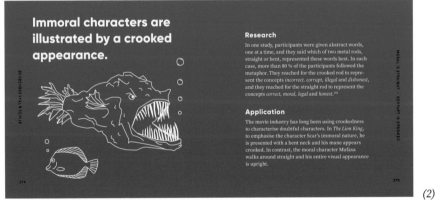

(2)

Each second double page (2) presents research indicating the intuitive nature of the metaphor.

It also shows examples of applying the metaphor that can be real or speculative.

15

The metaphors presented in this book may directly inspire your next design. They may also be used to reassess the metaphors used in current designs. Beyond this, they could also encourage you to listen to how people talk, to observe how they behave and to extract your own primary metaphors.[9]

Two caveats

The research we report in this book has been carefully selected and was taken from reputable scientific journals and conferences. However, the field is quite young and not all findings have been replicated so far. *Power posing*, for example, is a technique that makes you feel more powerful by assuming an expansive body posture. It has been shown to be a real effect many times over[10] – and many times not[11]. Similarly, although there is much evidence for **DANGEROUS IS ROUGH** being a primary metaphor,[12 13 14] its subconscious activation seems to fail when the metaphor is implemented in the context of interactive technology.[15]

Overall, it seems that people are able to consciously link physical properties and abstract ideas in the way primary metaphors suggest. The *subconscious* activation of metaphors, however, may depend on certain circumstances that are not yet fully understood. Which may be a relief when we think about it: we might fall less easily prey to subconscious manipulation!

The second caveat is that some primary metaphors may foster well-known stereotypes. When we thought that these would be too discriminating, we left these out of the book. With the remaining metaphors, it needs to be your conscious choice whether to design in line with the stereotype or against it. Making primary metaphors explicit may thus also inspire you to break up with existing stereotypes. It all depends on what you make of it!

1

BASIC UNITS

The number
of people living
in poverty
went down.

Die Kosten
sind gesunken.

広告のお陰で
売上が上がった。

MORE IS UP

LESS IS DOWN

Turn up the music!

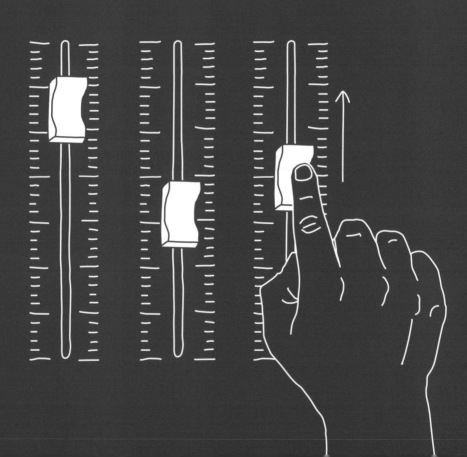

Research

Whether you add wine to your glass or put more books on a pile, levels go up. This natural connection between quantity and vertical extension is well learned and even applied to concepts that have no orientation in space. We talk about *rising inflation* and *falling prices* and immediately understand that there is now more inflation than before and that houses cost less. These patterns can be found in languages all over the world and they are internalised by almost everyone.[16]

Application

The best example is a volume slider. It is moved upwards to increase volume and downwards to decrease volume. Even without a label, users know how to use it. The same mapping could also be used for interacting with gestures. Wave your hands upwards to increase volume and downwards to decrease volume![17]

The shop is closed from 1 to 2 pm.

Die Veranstaltung geht von 12 bis 14 Uhr.

1時から2時まで休憩にしよう。

TIME IS
ON A PATH

In social media, posts move along a timeline.

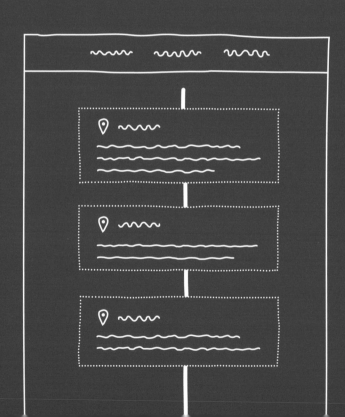

Research

We think of time as extending on a path. In Western cultures, this path is usually horizontal. We use it in writing and in gesture. When talking about future events, for example, we make forward or rightward gestures. When talking about past events, gestures go leftwards or backwards.[18] Arabic speakers, in contrast, tend to put past events in the front and future events behind[19] and for Mandarin speakers, the future is down and the past is up[20]. In most cases, the direction of the mapping can be explained by the dominant writing direction. In other cases, specific cultural preferences play a role.

Application

Historical diagrams extend the time from left to right. Calendars typically use timelines that extend rightwards and downwards. Analogue clocks feature a circular timeline. But time is always on a path.

Security forces were out in strength.

Die Initiative zielte auf einkommens-schwächere Familien.

不況の原因は需要の弱さにある。

MORE IS
STRONG

LESS IS
WEAK

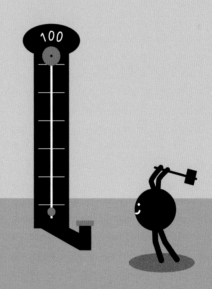

The stronger the touch, the louder the voice.

Research

Quantity and physical strength are related in everyday experience. The stronger you pull the lever on the handlebar, the more breaking power is applied to the wheel of your bike. Quantity and strength are also related in abstract thought. Researchers, for example, asked participants to express the concepts of *more* and *less* with strong and weak magnets. More than 90 % chose a strong over a weak magnet to express *more* and chose the weak magnet to express *less*.[21]

Application

This principle was employed in the art installation *What We Have Lost / What We Have Gained*. It presents a grid of video-projected mouths on a screen made of stretchy fabric. When physically pressed by a user, each video sample animates and sings a different vowel tone back to the player. The volume increases as the player presses stronger into the screen, physically distorting the display surface.[22]

Don't look
back in anger.

Schau nach
vorn, die
Zukunft liegt
vor Dir!

過去を振り返るのは
やめよう。

FUTURE
IS FRONT

PAST
IS BACK

Lean forwards to travel to the future!

Research

Movement through space is highly correlated with movement through time. Each next step moves us forwards. Going to a place where we have been before means going backwards. That the future is in front and the past is behind us is a highly generalised metaphor that can be found in language as well as in gestures.[23] In one study, participants wore a motion sensor while they imagined either past or future events with their eyes closed. Those who imagined past events were swaying slightly backwards and those who imagined future events moved slightly forwards with their bodies.[24]

Application

People know how to drive a Segway to move through space: just lean forwards or backwards to move forwards or backwards. Why not use a similar interaction to scroll through chronological data in virtual reality, like bank transactions, photos or social media timelines? What about maps that show how a city has been changing over time?

That was a
heated debate.

Heute bleibt
die Küche kalt.

利率が凍結された 。

ACTIVE IS WARM

INACTIVE IS COLD

Use heat maps
to show activity.

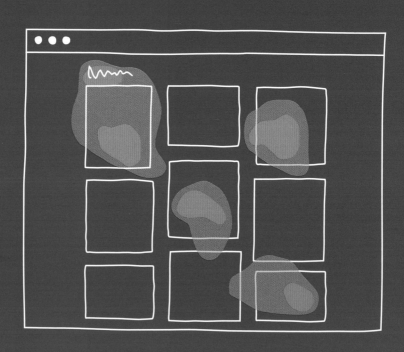

Research

Lizards are unable to regulate their body temperature, so they are active when it is warm and inactive when it is cold.[25] This relationship between temperature and activity extends to how we think and it is also valid when physical warmth is substituted by warm colours. Researchers found that people more often associate warm colours, like orange, red and yellow, with more activity and cool colours, like blue, green and purple, with less activity.[26]

Application

A heat map is a two-dimensional representation of data in which activity values are represented by colours. They can be used for visualising eye-tracking data or for visualising economic activity. Most commonly, cold colours stand for lower activity and warm colours stand for higher activity.

She was always
a light smoker.

Er spricht mit
leichtem Akzent.

軽く一杯飲もう。

MORE IS
HEAVY

LESS IS
LIGHT

Vision tricks your mind: Big things are not always heavy.

Research

Our expectation of how much things weigh relies heavily on our eyes.[27] A larger quantity of a certain material is bigger and will weigh more than a smaller quantity and thus we calibrate our grip and load forces accordingly.[28] Once the material is lifted, our motor system quickly adapts to potential misconceptions based on vision, but the overall expectation about the relationship between amount, size and weight remains persistent.

Application

In tangible user interfaces, quantity can be expressed by making tangibles heavier without needing to increase their size. This can be achieved by using denser materials or by using heavy, i.e. dark, colours.[29]

He just sails
through life.

Sie hat einen
eindrucksvollen
Lebenslauf.

人生山あり谷あり。

LIFE IS A JOURNEY
ON A PATH

Draw the path of your life for a better sense of purpose.

Research

According to psychologists, we need to have a sense of purpose and continuity in life to feel that it is meaningful.[30] Thinking about life in terms of a journey has many implications: goals are destinations; the self is the traveller; difficulties are impediments to motion; and a lack of purpose is a lack of direction. In one study, participants who wrote about their lives in terms of a journey judged their lives to be more purposeful and satisfying than others who were not using the journey metaphor.[31] In another study, participants who visualised events from their past as physical locations on a path also perceived a higher sense of continuity in their lives than others.[32]

Application

The effects of the journey metaphor are stronger when people are uncertain about their own identity and when they experience life as incoherent. This opens opportunities for using the journey metaphor for psychotherapeutic counselling.

He's like
something
out of the last
century.

Ihr Morgen
war extrem
vollgepackt.

彼はまるで
江戸時代から
抜け出してきた
ような人だ。

TIME PERIODS
ARE CONTAINERS

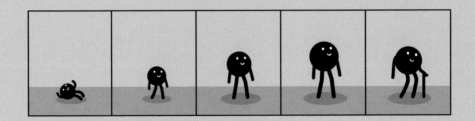

Programme your heating periods with containers.

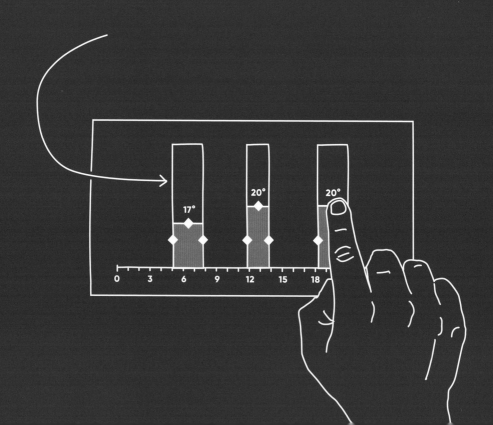

Research

When programming your central heating controller, you may want to set the heating to run, for example, for fixed time periods in the morning, at midday and in the evening. Currently, for each of the timeslots, you would programme a beginning and an end time. In one study, researchers designed a heating system that could be programmed visually by moving time containers and their boundaries on a timeline. The user interface was faster and more intuitive to use than the typical system available on the market at that time.[33]

Application

Information graphics often show different time periods as different containers: dynasties of monarchs, phases of war and political stability, and geological aeons.

There is no turning back when the blossom has fallen.

Wir drehen die Zeit zurück in das Jahr 1960.

あなたの先回りをするつもりはないのですが…。

NOVEL IS
CLOCKWISE

OLD-FASHIONED IS
ANTICLOCKWISE

Rotating an object clockwise opens you up to new experiences.

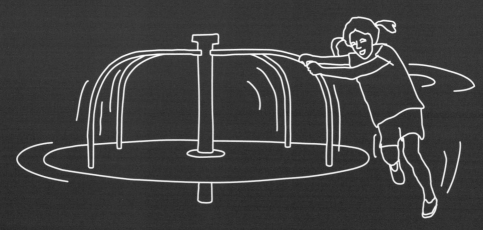

Research

Researchers could show that seemingly meaningless rotations of our hands in a clockwise direction shape our orientation towards novelty. For example, people prefer more unusual flavours of jelly beans such as popcorn or punch over conventional flavours such as strawberry or lemon after performing a clockwise rotation movement. This movement also increases their self-reported attitude towards novelty in a personality test.[34]

Application

Rotations are omnipresent in our environment: door knobs, keyholes, rotating doors, bottle caps, fortune wheels, rotary knobs on electronic devices. Can entering a revolving door in a clockwise direction make us more innovative?

This is such
a big class!

Die Klasse ist
größer als die
andere.

このクラスは
あのクラスより
大きい。

MORE IS
BIG

LESS IS
SMALL

How big or small is the number?

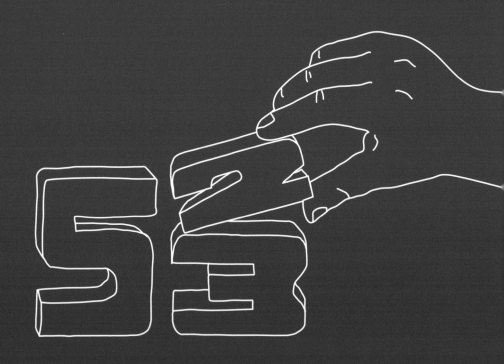

Research

Quantity and size are correlated in the physical world: more sheets of paper make a larger stack and more rain water makes larger puddles. Quantity and size are also linked in more abstract concepts: we expect larger objects (in our physical environment or on a screen) to represent higher quantities: more time, more responsibility, more money and so on.[35] [36] [37]

Application

We recognise numbers more easily when numerical size and visual size correspond. For example, in a long line of numbers, a *2* will be understood more easily when it is smaller than a *6* next to it.[38] Applying this in data visualisation could therefore make large numerical data sets more comprehensible to humans. The same idea is realised in special building blocks for elementary school children. These blocks teach the size of a number through their corresponding physical sizes.[39]

2

BASIC JUDGEMENTS

He has a big heart.

Sie spielt ganz großen Fußball.

彼は器の大きな人物だ。

GOOD
IS BIG

BAD
IS SMALL

Big is good – bigger is better!

Research

When offered two pieces of cake – would you really choose the smaller one? The association of *big is good – bigger is better* is rooted so deeply that it even works with font sizes. In one experiment, participants identified positive words in a large font faster than positive words in a small font. In another experiment, participants rated neutral words as more positive when they were written in a larger font.[40]

Application

In China's casino capital Macau you can observe how simple labels on a game of Cussec bias gamblers' betting behaviour. In Cussec, gamblers can bet on *big* and *small*, which refer to the total value of three dice thrown. Both bets have equal chances of winning. Gamblers, however, bet more frequently on *big* and less frequently on *small*. They also estimate their likelihood of winning to be higher when they have chosen *big*.[41]

He was no good with soft words.

Wir haben ein paar harte Jahre hinter uns.

あいつは頭が固い。

PLEASANT
IS SOFT

UNPLEASANT
IS HARD

Soft cuddles give greater well-being.

Research

Usually, we regard soft touches to be more pleasant than hard touches. This association between the pleasurable and the soft can also be found in the brain. The same brain region, the orbitofrontal cortex, is activated when doing pleasurable things like eating fatty food – and being touched with a velvety piece of fabric, for example.[42]

Application

Soft animal robots (e.g. the robot seal PARO) have been used in hospitals, nursing homes and other care facilities to enhance the mental and physical well-being of elderly people.[43] Touching and petting these animals reduces tension and helps relaxation, because the soft contact fosters the production of endorphins.[44] This may also explain why people prefer robots that feel like plush teddy bears over those that feel like scaly reptiles.

Don't play so
roughly with
the baby.

Die See ist
rau.

この犬は気性が荒い。

DANGEROUS IS ROUGH

SAFE IS SMOOTH

Beware when the ride is feeling bumpy!

Research

Experiences of danger and roughness are strongly intertwined. Potentially troublesome and dangerous places, for example, are described as being rough (e.g. *rough pubs*).[45] Studies in Canada and Germany have shown that most people associate the word *dangerous* with rough objects and the word *safe* with smooth objects.[46 47]

Application

Vevey, a city in Switzerland, covered the railing of a tall bridge with a rough material, similar to sand paper. The height of the bridge and the rough texture of the railing immediately convey a feeling of danger. On highways, road safety features like speed bumps and rumble strips apply roughness to make potential dangers more obvious to drivers.

That's a big
discovery!

Er hält sich
an kleinen
Details auf.

小さな過ちは
誰にでもある。

**IMPORTANT
IS BIG**

**UNIMPORTANT
IS SMALL**

75

The most important function? Make it big!

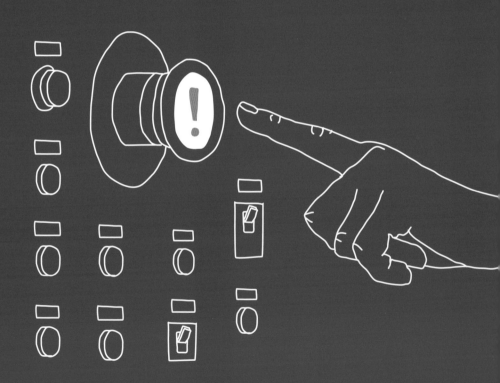

Research

When people are asked to sketch a USB stick that contains important information, they draw a bigger shape compared to when the USB stick contains expired or no information at all.[48]

Application

The most important functions often have the largest controls – be it the snooze button on the alarm clock or the emergency stop on a machine tool. Users also prefer larger widgets for more important functions, e.g. a giant slider for setting the federal interest rate versus the interest rate for just one branch of a bank.[49]

She has chosen the right path.

So wie dieser Tisch aussieht, hat der Schreiner wohl zwei linke Hände.

家業が左前になる。

BAD IS LEFT

GOOD IS RIGHT

Why do some people point left with their right hand?

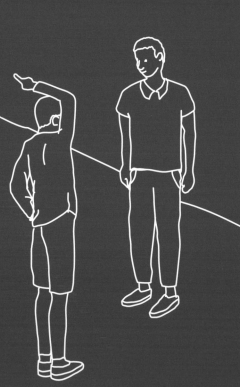

Research

Right-handed politicians gesture more with their right hand when talking about positive topics and more with their left hand when talking about negative topics.[50] In many countries, the left hand is reserved for activities considered dirty.[51] Ghanaians, for example, avoid giving directions with their left hand – even if it means assuming awkward postures when pointing left.[52]

Application

With the widespread use of personal computers, people have become well trained in touch typing. It can be shown that words that are mainly typed with the right hand are perceived more positively than words mainly typed with the left hand. As a consequence, even the names given to newborns have become biased towards the right-hand side of the keyboard.[53]

These colours
are close,
but not the
same.

Produktivität
und Löhne
laufen immer
weiter aus-
einander.

私の立場に
一番近いのは
あなたです。

DIFFERENT IS FAR

SIMILAR IS NEAR

Come a step closer and we might agree.

Research

We tend to interpret closeness as similarity and we tend to sketch similar things closer together. When two persons are depicted as being near to one another, people think that they have similar political views. Likewise, when cities are described as being similar, people draw them closer together on a map than cities described as being dissimilar.[54]

Application

Similar things tend to occur close together in the natural environment: flowers, trees, rocks, insects and gregarious animals. World regions that are close to each other tend to be more similar, e.g. in climate, landscape, linguistic dialects, flora and fauna.[55] As with regions, so it is in supermarkets: similar items are on the same shelf. Although we would not like to see sanitary towels next to sausages, barbecue items like steaks, tongs, and lighters go well together.

What is central here?

Was ist die Kernaussage ihrer Rede?

枝葉末節にとらわれすぎではないか?

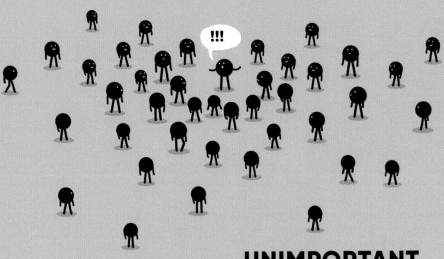

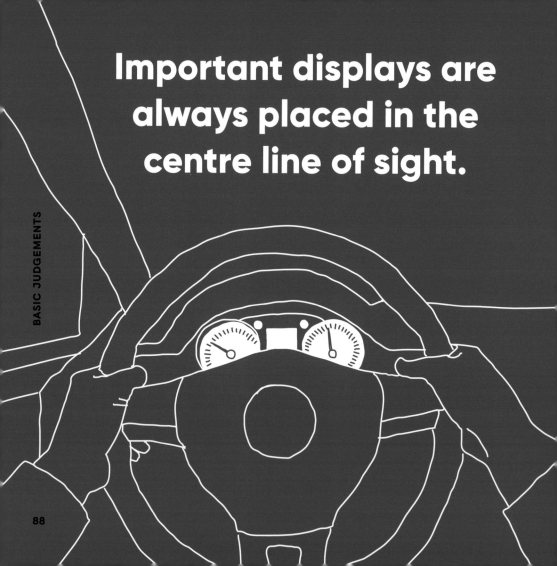

Important displays are always placed in the centre line of sight.

Research

When people make touch gestures on mobile phones, 95% move their index finger towards the centre of the screen to indicate something important, and they move their finger towards the periphery of the screen to indicate something unimportant. When gesturing with the whole phone, they move the phone towards themselves to show that something is important and away from their body to show that something is unimportant.[56]

Application

Important instrumentation in cars and airplane cockpits is always in the centre line of sight. Displays and controls of lesser importance tend to be more in the periphery.

Although she usually got on well with children, she found Hilary heavy going.

Die Reparatur war ganz leicht.

こんな簡単な計算問題、軽いもんさ。

DIFFICULT IS HEAVY

EASY IS LIGHT

Develop super-powers by using white moving boxes!

Research

Heavy objects are usually difficult to handle. To create the feeling of difficulty, thus, add physical weight to an object – or just paint it in a darker colour. Psychologists prepared boxes with an identical weight but in different colours, e.g. darker and lighter versions of green and violet. As expected, people rated the dark-coloured boxes as heavier and they associated these more with the concept of *difficulty* than the bright-coloured boxes.[57]

Application

Lifting heavy objects is easier when they are painted in a lighter colour. Japanese scientists created augmented reality glasses that could re-colour objects. Wearing these glasses, people showed greater endurance in lifting dumbbells when these were re-coloured in white rather than in black.[58] Would difficult maths problems also appear easier to solve when viewed through these glasses?

We hit a peak
last year, but it's
been downhill
ever since.

Spitzenleistung!

昨年ピークを
迎えましたが、
それ以来ずっと
下り坂です。

**GOOD
IS UP**

**BAD
IS DOWN**

95

Properties up north in the city are for the affluent.

Research

GOOD IS UP – BAD IS DOWN is deeply embedded into our thinking. In one experiment, participants identified positive words faster at the top of a computer screen and negative words faster at the bottom of the screen.[59] In another experiment, participants remembered the position of positive images to be higher and that of negative images to be lower than the position in which the images were originally shown.[60]

Application

Retailers place expensive, high-quality brands on the top shelves and cheaper brands on the bottom shelves. Products displayed at the top in supermarkets are more frequently noted, considered and bought by customers.[61] Even more strikingly, when no further information is given, people prefer properties in the northern area of a city and believe that the poor are more likely to live in a southern area.[62]

He always creates those smooth contour-less designs.

Das lief einfach zu glatt.

この人物は、
激動の時代を生き、
波瀾万丈の
人生を送った。

EXCITING IS
ROUGH

BORING IS
SMOOTH

**Smooth rides
make boring stories.**

Research

People associate images of rough landscapes with exciting activities that are fun and enjoyable. They associate images of smooth landscapes with tameness, familiarity, peace and relaxation.[63] Similarly, the aesthetic appreciation of landscapes differentiates between the *beautiful* and the *picturesque*. The *beautiful* is often seen as smooth, e.g. a well-tended garden or a beautiful castle. The *picturesque* has elements of roughness, e.g. untamed nature and decay. Thus, a castle in ruins can be more exciting than an intact building.

Application

It was excitement through the picturesque that the tourists of the 18th century were seeking and that landscape architects were trying to simulate.[64] In general, when designers create a visual language for a project, the level of excitement (or peacefulness) of the content can be regulated through the level of roughness (or smoothness) of what is shown.

Don't attach
any weight to
those rumours.

Sie fällte ein
schwerwiegendes
Urteil.

当局は
その事件を
重く見た。

IMPORTANT

IS HEAVY

UNIMPORTANT

IS LIGHT

Heavy books seem more important.

Research

People perceive that books, USB sticks or hard drives weigh more when these contain personally or financially important information.[65] Similarly, holding something heavy can influence our judgement of how important it is. When reviewing resumes for a job position, for example, participants who read these on heavier clipboards rated the candidates as better suited for the job and thought that they displayed more serious interest in the position.[66] Holding onto heavy objects also makes people think harder. When holding heavy clipboards, participants show less agreement with weak arguments, consider fair procedures as more important and are more confident about their opinion than when holding a light clipboard.[67]

Application

Would heavier pens, garments or backpacks enhance decision making in complex situations?

The course of true love never ran smoothly.

Das ist ja nochmal glatt gegangen.

まったく
人使いの
荒い人だ。

UNPLEASANT
IS ROUGH

PLEASANT
IS SMOOTH

Rough architecture expels the homeless from the cities.

Research

In a prominent study, psychologists let people solve a five-piece puzzle, either a version covered in rough sandpaper or a version with smooth pieces. The participants then read a story describing an ambiguous social interaction between two people. Those who worked with the rough puzzle were more likely to describe the interaction as unpleasant, uncoordinated and harsh. Those working with the smooth puzzle, however, described the interaction as more pleasant, coordinated and friendly.[68]

Application

Unpleasant Design is concerned with deterring unwanted people from lingering in public places, for example in front of shop windows. One strategy is to make surfaces rough and spiky so that they become too unpleasant to sit or lie down on for more than a short time.[69] This example reminds us that design decisions are political: who gets to decide who is welcome and who is not?

3

EMOTIONS

She is a light-hearted girl.

Der Besuch brachte etwas Erleichterung. Danach versank er wieder in Schwermut.

休み明けの仕事は気が重い。

SAD IS HEAVY

HAPPY IS LIGHT

Depression is like a heavy weight on the shoulders.

Research

We tend to associate heavy objects more with sadness and light objects more with happiness.[70] We also rate dark (heavy) colours as sad and bright (light) colours as happy.[71] Indeed, the mood of Instagram users can be revealed by the type of photo filters they use. Healthy people are more likely to choose filters that lighten the colours of a photograph. Depressive people tend to apply filters that darken the photo.[72]

Application

People suffering from depression often talk about their condition as a burden. Hence, the outcome of psychotherapy can be predicted by a change in the metaphors patients use. When burden metaphors are transformed into unloading metaphors like "I feel like things are getting lighter" or "the pressure has lifted", the psychotherapy is likely to have a positive outcome. When the metaphors do not change, the therapy is more likely to have a negative outcome.[73]

I'm feeling up today.

Kopf hoch!

愛犬を亡くしてから、ずっと気落ちしている。

HAPPY
IS UP

SAD IS
DOWN

How does a sad robot sound?

Research

If someone is sad, their head is hanging down. A cross-cultural study shows that this emotional expression is internationally valid: Japanese, Sri Lankan and American participants recognised the postures of a digital manikin as sadness, when its head and arms were hanging down.[74]

Application

Musical pitch is also mapped to vertical space. Thus, to express sadness in a robot, it can make a falling beeping sound, helping users to identify the robot's emotional state.[75]

That warmed
my spirits.

Freude schöner
Götterfunken ...

悲しくて
身も心も
凍えそうだ。

HAPPY IS WARM

SAD IS COLD

Happy despite cold and rainy weather?

Research

Happiness and sadness are closely related to our bodily experience of temperature. In a psychological experiment, researchers filled jars with warm or cold water. Participants associated the experience of warm jars with happiness and cold jars with sadness.[76] Similarly, warm (i.e. reddish) colours are associated with happiness and cold (i.e. blueish) colours are associated with sadness.[77]

Application

The effects of warm-cold colour associations may be used to bias people's judgements.[78] For example, would people be happier with cold and rainy weather if they wore orange-tinted glasses?

After the violent
argument he
felt empty.

Ich fühle eine
Leere in mir.

虚無感で涙が
止まらない。

**HAPPY
IS FULL**

**SAD IS
EMPTY**

Eating more because you feel empty?

Research

Psychologists have found that overeating can be a compensation strategy for feelings of emptiness. When participants watched a frightening film, the resulting negative emotions like anxiety and sadness triggered overeating in those who were on a diet.[79] Depression, too, can affect eating habits. Some patients have a decreased appetite, while others experience an increase in emotional eating.[80]

Application

To counter feelings of emptiness, psychotherapists could use the metaphor. Their patients could add a marble to a glass for every meaningful activity they are engaged in. The increasingly filling container reminds the patients that their lives can become fulfilling again.

A bright future.

Es gibt durch-
aus Lichtblicke.

彼には暗い過去が
あるらしい。

HAPPY IS
BRIGHT

SAD IS
DARK

129

How to turn on the light without touching a switch.

Research

As suggested by the expression *bright smile*, researchers have shown that people judge smiling faces as appearing brighter than frowning faces.[81] Similarly, when people feel sad and hopeless, they perceive ambient light as darker. Sad people thus may have a need for more ambient lighting.[82]

Application

As social robots become increasingly popular, designers explore how robots can express emotions. To communicate happiness and sadness in a robot way, a happy robot could display bright colours (e.g. yellow) and a sad robot could display dark colours (e.g. blue). People can match these emotions to coloured light with over 80% accuracy.[83]

He was a shy, timid man whose lust for life was overshadowed by fear.

Eine düstere Vorahnung kam in ihr auf.

隣国との関係に暗雲が立ち込めてきた。

FEAR IS
DARKNESS

133

The dark is #5 on the list of children's greatest fears.[84]

Research

Humans perceive their environment mainly visually. As vision requires light we see less in the dark. Seeing less means knowing less about the surroundings, resulting in a fear of stumbling or of overlooking hidden dangers. Hence, darkness has become a symbol of ignorance, fear and evil. The Christian Bible is a witness of this connection: "When I looked for good, then evil came unto me: and when I waited for light there came darkness" (Job 30.26).

Application

Well-lit streets can reduce fears at night. Research shows that we feel safer walking along roads that are properly illuminated at night.[85]

They backed down after seeing the superior opponent.

Wir schreckten davor zurück, die Wanderung bei diesem Wetter zu wagen.

恐怖で腰が引けてしまった。

FEAR IS
REPULSION

Push to get rid of the spiders.

Research

People fearful of spiders keep away from spiders. Only if forced do they approach them very slowly. In one study, participants responded to spider and non-spider pictures by pulling a joystick towards themselves or by pushing it away from themselves. People fearful of spiders responded to spider pictures more quickly when pushing than when pulling. The effect also occurred when participants only had to indicate which orientation the spider picture was in (i.e., landscape or portrait).[86]

Application

How can a robot express fear? It appears that moving backwards is the best way to signal that a robot feels fear – even better than using sound or colour as communication channels.[87]

He makes my
blood boil.

Sie musste
erstmal Dampf
ablassen.

彼は烈火のごとく、
かんかんに
怒っている。

ANGER IS HEAT

The English explode like volcanos and the Chinese let off steam.

Research

In many cultures, anger is strongly associated with heat.[88] Whereas the Chinese associate anger with hot air, the English associate it with a hot fluid.[89] This might be because for Westerners, water is the source of life and for the Chinese, air or *qi* is the source of the universe.[90]

Application

Designers often need to convey emotions in a design, for example in social robots, pictures, apps and websites. Representing anger can become difficult to realise if things need to heat up physically. An easier way is to use the colour red, which most people associate with heat – and anger.[91]

4

SOCIAL RELATIONS

A warm welcome to you all!

Er zeigte ihr die kalte Schulter.

新入生を温かく迎え入れる。

FRIENDLY IS WARM

UNFRIENDLY IS COLD

People who are given a warm mug tend to see their environment as friendlier than those with a cold one.

Research

Holding a warm beverage makes people feel emotionally closer to a known other person and leads them to judge strangers as being friendlier and warmer.[92] Also, the surrounding room temperature can influence how close people feel to others.[93] Similarly, when people are socially excluded they not only feel bad but also their skin gets colder. Then, a warm cup of tea helps them to recover from their negative feelings.[94]

Application

Imagine people are playing a serious game about immigration using a *thermouse*, a mouse-like input device that can change temperature?[95] Would those playing with a warm mouse show more inclusive attitudes than those playing with a cold mouse? And, could warm mugs and pocket warmers give some relief in situations where people feel lonely or socially anxious?

Her way
of talking is
rough.

Er ist ein
glatter Typ.

彼は言葉遣いが荒い。

POLITE
IS SMOOTH

IMPOLITE
IS ROUGH

151

Foam blocks can be polite, too.

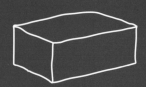

Research

Researchers gave participants two foam blocks – one with a smooth and one with a rough surface. When asked which of the blocks they associated with *polite* and which with *impolite*, 95% associated the smooth block with *polite* and the rough block with *impolite*.[96]

Application

Not only the smoothness of an object but also the external appearance of a person can imply a sense of politeness. Imagine, for example, the look of a business consultant. One would expect a well-ironed rather than a crumpled blouse, a clean-shaven rather than a stubble

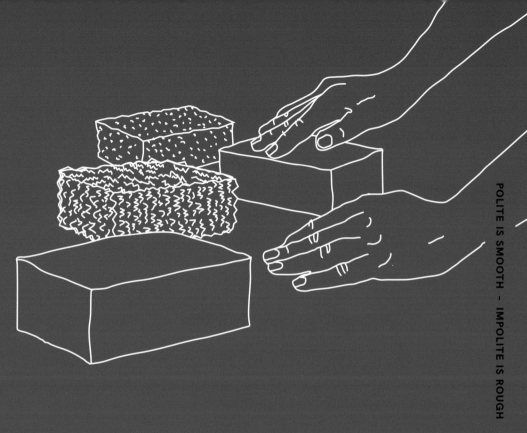

chin and polished shoes rather than worn-out ones. But this is a case where metaphors can foster thinking in stereotypes. Thus, pay attention when people with curly, frizzy hair or uneven, wrinkly skins are discriminated against when applying for customer-facing jobs.

153

She and my father were distant with each other.

Sie ist seine engste Vertraute.

彼とは近しい間柄だ。

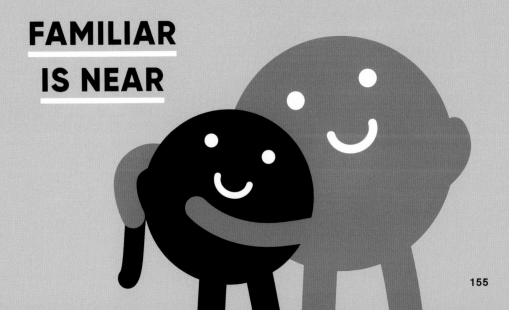

UNFAMILIAR
IS FAR

FAMILIAR
IS NEAR

Becoming friends
by chance.

Research

Just marking near or far points on a sheet of paper can change our perception of familiarity. In one study, after marking points that were further away on a diagram, participants reported weaker bonds to their siblings, parents and hometown than participants who had marked points closer to each other.[97]

Application

Physical proximity, even by chance, helps with making new friends. At a university introductory session, freshers were randomly assigned seats in the lecture room. Students who sat next to each other or in the same row found each other more attractive than those who sat further away. The session had profound long-lasting effects. One year later, those who had been sitting closer to each other were more likely to be friends and rated the intensity of their friendship higher than those who sat further away.[98]

I`m touched.

Sein Liebes-
bekenntnis hat
mich berührt.

その言葉は
心に触れた。

EMOTIONAL INTIMACY IS
PHYSICAL CONTACT

Touching through machines: how real does it feel?

Research

How nice would it be to touch a loved one when feeling lonely in a hotel room on a business trip far away? Computers can make it possible. But can touching through a device substitute for a real touch? Researchers in Singapore asked students to watch a sad movie and then they compared their physiological responses when being directly touched by their partners or tele-touched by a stranger. The partner's touch alleviated the participants' sadness more than the stranger's tele-touch. The tele-touch, however, was better than not being touched at all.[99]

Application

Huggy Pajama is a wearable system that enables parents and children to hug one another over a distance. The parent's device is a small doll that is able to sense pressure and sends hug signals to the child's haptic jacket. Through inflatable air chambers the jacket simulates the feeling of being hugged.[100] *Kissenger* (kiss messenger) is a robotic gadget that can physically simulate a kiss to strengthen intimacy over long distances.[101] In its latest version, it can be combined with a smartphone so that kissers can see their loved ones while they are kissing them.

She is my
better half.

Sie sind ein
Herz und
eine Seele.

夫婦は一心同体だ。

LOVE IS A UNITY
OF PARTS

We are one.

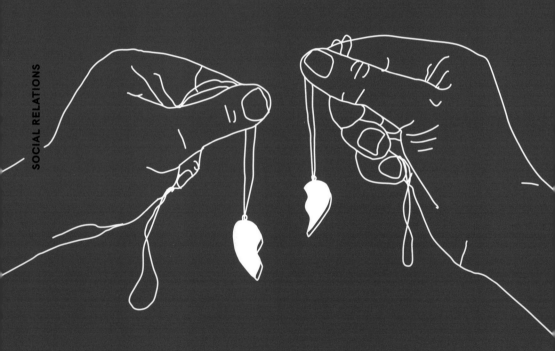

Research

According to the world literature, romantic love is based on the concept of unity, a state in which, at the height of passion, the desire of the lovers is to be united and to dissolve all distance between them. Love increases oxytocin, a hormone important for bonding between partners. Love triggers the brain's reward system and deactivates regions associated with critical social assessment and negative emotions.[102]

Application

Love is often physically conveyed as a unity of parts. Couples may wear matching parts of a necklace or a heart locket containing pictures of their partners.

Our relationship has gotten off track.

Wir müssen nun getrennte Wege gehen.

夫婦として同じ道を歩んでいこう。

LOVE IS A JOURNEY

The love that came
to be ...

Research

We use the structure of journeys to metaphorically understand the domain of love and love relationships. Lovers are travellers, the relationship is the vehicle, and the progress made is the distance covered. These mappings carry new meaning and can create new expectations. Research found that a couple's relationship is less affected by conflicts when the partners think of love as a journey instead of a unity of parts.[103]

Application

The metaphor is reflected in the lyrics of love songs, for example in *Vision of Love* by Mariah Carey. Here, the line "the love that came to be" indicates that love can come from a certain place: it comes into existence and can develop into something significant. Correspondingly, the lovers travel great distances to find love, both geographically and emotionally. This is illustrated by the line "to the one that was waiting for me" from the same song.[104]

He fell ill.

Sie ist topfit.

風邪でダウンしている。

HEALTHY IS UP

SICK IS DOWN

Sick mammals lie down, healthy ones stand up.

Research

Most mammals lie down when they feel sick and get up again as they recover. Humans also associate illness with being down. Patients with conversion disorder, for example, experience their bodies as ill, although physical examinations reveal negative results. Researchers found that these patients reacted faster to body-related words (e.g. *arm*) when these were presented at the bottom of a screen compared to when they were presented at the top. This downward bias for body-related words did not appear with non-body words (e.g. *clock*), and it was stronger the more somatic symptoms the patients reported.[105]

Application

In user interfaces, games or information graphics, healthiness can be illustrated by standing up and sickness by sitting or lying characters. However, try to be thoughtful with your message: wheelchair users, for example, do not stand but they are not (automatically) sick.

She's working
against the
big boys in
industry.

Die Anliegen
der kleinen
Leute müssen
mitbedacht
werden.

巨大な権力に
立ち向かう。

POWERFUL
IS BIG

POWERLESS
IS SMALL

Power-up with power posing.

Research

Technology sometimes forces people into expansive postures, for example, when standing and interacting with a large wall-mounted display. Sometimes they assume contracting postures, for example, when sitting and interacting with a smartphone. Research has shown that assuming expansive postures can make us feel more powerful[106] but it can also increase dishonest and immoral behaviour. People in expansive postures are thus more likely to steal money, cheat on a test, commit traffic violations[107] and keep monetary benefits to themselves.[108]

Application

It is easy to recognise the powerful. They tend to drive larger cars, sit in larger offices and generally tend to occupy more space with their bodies. In organisation charts, often the names of executives are printed in larger type, with the names of subordinate managers in smaller type.

He is a hard taskmaster.

Die Richterin fällte ein hartes Urteil.

固く禁止する。

**STRICT
IS HARD**

**FLEXIBLE
IS SOFT**

Soft pillows for world peace?

Research

If people are seated on a hard wooden chair versus a soft-cushioned one, they are less likely to change from their initial decisions when asked to review them. For example, once given an offer price for a new car, this decision is less malleable when sitting on a hard chair than when sitting on a soft chair.[109]

Application

As people can be influenced by the seat of their pants, sitting on cushions might lead to a more compromising course in political negotiations. Maybe negotiation rooms everywhere should be equipped with softer cushions for the benefit of world peace?

There is a
severe social
imbalance in
the city.

Wir müssen
die sozialen
Ungleichheiten
ausbalancieren.

社会の不均衡を
正さねばならない。

SOCIAL JUSTICE
IS BALANCE

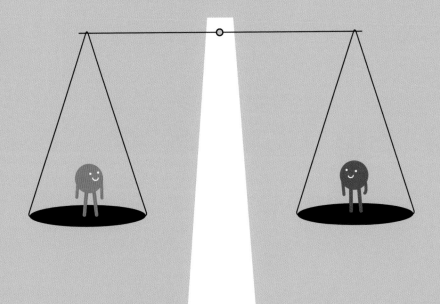

Get in balance with your social environment.

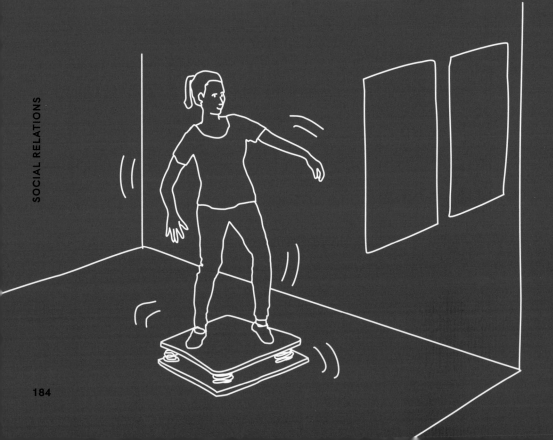

Research

In an interactive installation called *springboard*, design researchers presented two pictures next to each other about social justice topics like community safety, housing or food production. Participants were required to "bring the issue represented by the pictures into balance". A wobbly platform held by mattress springs served as the input device for this task. It had to be operated by shifting the balance of the whole body. After interacting with the spring-board, participants had higher awareness of issues of social justice and were also more willing to take action, compared to participants who only used conventional slider controllers.[110]

Application

Schools could use interactive installations like *springboard* to raise awareness of inequality, to evoke empathy and to trigger discussions about issues of social justice.

In April,
the political
tensions turned
hot again.

Die Grenze war
ein Krisenherd
mit einigen
schwelenden
Konflikten.

両国間には常に
争いの火種が
くすぶっている。

CONFLICT

IS HEAT

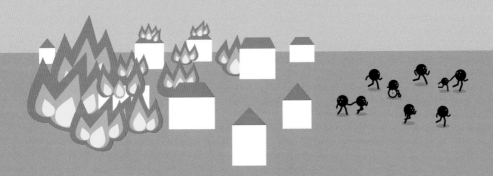

Hotter cities are more violent.

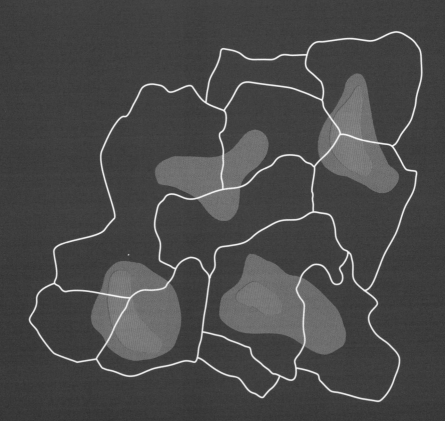

Research

There is ample evidence that physical heat is connected with conflict, aggression and violence. Hotter cities
are more violent than cooler cities.[111] Rates of assaults,
spontaneous riots and spouse battering are higher
during hotter days, months, seasons and years. There
are more murders and assaults during the summer; hot
summers have more violence than cooler summers;
and violence rates are higher in hotter years than in
cooler years.[112]

Application

The association between conflict and heat is often used
in data visualisations, especially of war reports and
maps of regions in crisis. Hot or warm colours (e.g. red,
orange) are used to indicate regions of strong conflict.

5

KNOWLEDGE & COMMUNICATION

Is there any-
thing you can
tell us that may
shed light
on his death?

Sie ist ein helles
Köpfchen.

事情に暗いので
黙っていた 。

KNOWING IS BRIGHT

UNKNOWING IS DARK

193

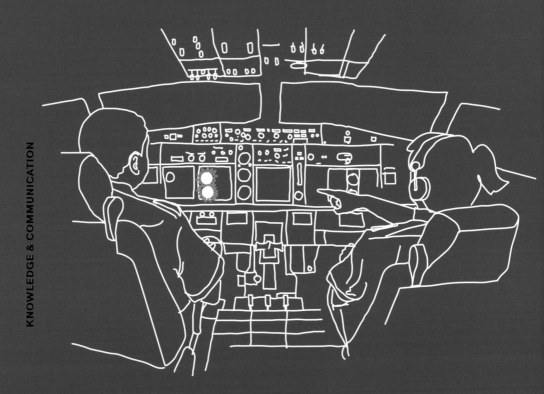

**See? That's
what I mean.**

Research

People are primarily visual animals. In the dark, we cannot see and thus are prone to stumbling and falling over. This leads us to associate brightness with knowledge, wisdom and good, and the dark with ignorance, fear and evil.[113] The metaphor generalises to intelligence as a personality trait: there are *bright physicists* and *dim-witted radicals*. Experiments have shown, for example, that images of open books with bright backgrounds are rated as more likely to represent works of genius than books with darker backgrounds.[114]

Application

When *fly-by-wire* concepts emerged, human-centred aircraft design turned to the *dark cockpit* philosophy. The cockpit displays should remain *dark and quiet* – unless there is something the pilot needs to know or pay attention to. Then that specific control will light up and show its information. Although widespread, this design philosophy has been criticised. If there is a serious incident, there is too much information in the dark for the pilot to get a proper overview of the situation.

Far be it from
me to stand
in the path of
true love.

Sie legten ihm
nahe, die Stadt
zu verlassen.

消費増税は
身近なテーマだ。

NOT
CONSIDERED
IS FAR

CONSIDERED
IS NEAR

197

Put the important things where you can't overlook them.

Research

Things that are near the current focus of attention will have a greater chance to be considered than items that are further away. When observing student work teams, for example, researchers saw that students placed objects that were not task-relevant further away from themselves and they were more likely to interact with nearby things, e.g. books or a laptop computer. When observing people preparing their medication, researchers saw that patients placed their pills near a glass of water to make sure that they remembered to take these pills during breakfast.[115]

Application

This metaphor is a central guideline in user interface design. Here, it is known as the *proximity compatibility principle*. It specifies that when users need to integrate multiple sources of information, their performance will be best when that information is displayed close together.[116]

Their chief
strength is
technology.

Das war
eine schwache
Leistung.

彼は交渉に強い。

COMPETENT
IS STRONG

INCOMPETENT
IS WEAK

Strong Body, Strong Mind?

Research

Research has found that physical fitness and fluid intelligence are related. Fluid intelligence is the ability to think logically and solve problems in novel situations. This competence is higher in the physically fit and it can be enhanced by physical training.[117]

Application

Handgrip strength can be used to predict cognitive decline in older adults. When handgrip strength decreases over time it is more likely that people suffer from cognitive losses when becoming older. Similarly, a strong handgrip indicates cognitive resources may be conserved.[118]

The fieldworker does not look at society from afar; he observes the phenomena at a detailed level.

Lass uns das mal mit Abstand betrachten.

君の考えは
手に取るように
わかる。

ABSTRACT

IS FAR

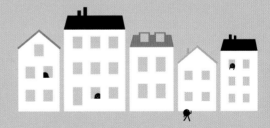

CONCRETE

IS NEAR

Keeping your distance makes you more creative.

Research

In two experiments, people solved riddles or engaged in creative tasks. One group was told that the riddles or tasks were produced in a nearby location, e.g. their home town. Another group was told that these were produced in a place further away, e.g. a different country. As abstract thought is required in creative problem solving, people who believed that their task originated from a far rather than a close location could solve more riddles and produced more creative responses.[119]

Application

People prefer stock performance data that are averaged over larger time intervals (e.g. monthly rather than daily) when the stock is traded on a distant stock exchange rather than a nearby stock exchange.[120] These findings have important practical implications for financial decision making because the intervals in which stock data are presented dramatically influence the trends that are visible.

I firmly rely
on him.

Ich gebe
nur etwas auf
harte Fakten.

私は彼の無実を
固く信じている。

CERTAIN
IS HARD

UNCERTAIN
IS SOFT

Soft assurance or soft uncertainty?

Research

When people face uncertainty, e.g. on the political and economic level, they like to touch soft things like soft-grip pens, plush toys or soft candy.[121] These soft haptic sensations are comforting and help to reduce uncertainty on subsequent tasks. When uncertainty is not the focus, soft objects can trigger feelings of uncertainty. In one study, participants sitting on a wobbly inflatable seat cushion rather than a rigid one perceived their romantic relationships to be less likely to last. The more people felt physically unstable and off-balance, the more they reported feeling uncertain, confused and lacking in confidence.[122]

Application

Soft fidgets can be used to comfort people in stressful situations and to cope with uncertainty. In some situations, they could also protect us from being overconfident. What if we had a soft overlay on the keyboard: would this prevent us from writing rude Twitter messages?

I am filled with information.

Das waren nur leere Worte.

彼はいつも
新しいアイデアで
いっぱいだ。

**HAVING ENOUGH
RELEVANT INFORMATION
IS BEING FULL**

**LACKING
RELEVANCE IS
BEING EMPTY**

Can you check all the boxes?

Research

Our ability to process information is restricted as our working memory can hold only around seven chunks of information.[123] Thus, the memory-container is quickly filled and can easily overflow. Research needs to find out both how we can enhance our capacities and how we can reduce or compact the streams of information to fit in.[124]

Application

When we use online forms, many interface elements only convey meaningful information when they are filled in (e.g. text boxes). When clicking checkboxes and radio buttons, their graphical representations appear filled when selected and empty when deselected.

She was a lady of strong character.

Gegen seinen starken Cha-rakter kam man kaum an.

自信が人を強くする。

**CONFIDENT
IS STRONG**

**UNCONFIDENT
IS WEAK**

Have a workout
before you pitch.

Research

Being confident means to be less influenced by external forces and to have the strength to endure potentially negative circumstances. Thus, people associate confidence with strength. This association can also be found in behavioural studies. For example, when participants were asked to express the concepts of confidence or shyness, 80% behaved as predicted by the metaphor. They chose a strong over a weak magnet to express confidence and chose the weak magnet to express shyness.[125]

Application

Force Touch (aka *3D Touch*) was developed by Apple. When implemented, touchscreens can distinguish between light and strong touch events. People could use it to express their confidence in their actions. A strong (versus weak) touch could mean: delete this email (versus archive it); put this event into my calendar (versus pencil it in); or skip this video (versus fast-forward it).

The writer did a wonderful job of transporting me into the worlds of elves and goblins.

Die Geschichte zog mich sofort in ihren Bann.

彼の生き生きとした語り口で、物語の世界に引き込まれてしまった。

NARRATIVE ABSORPTION IS ATTRACTION INTO THE STORY CONTAINER

Let's plunge into a new story!

Research

When we watch a film, read a novel or play a video game, we may experience *narrative absorption*. How we talk and think about narrative absorption is linked to a physical force acting from a distance that draws us closer into a *story container*.[126] We are dragged or transported into another world. We follow the characters; we get caught up in their lives; we are fully immersed in their story. Even the technical terms emphasise this experience. Experts in film, literature and video games talk about *transportation*, *involvement* and *immersion*.

Application

There are countless ways to enhance the feeling of plunging in while reading, playing, watching, listening, studying or just daydreaming. Of course, 3D-movies and VR-glasses create a strong feeling of immersion. But also putting people into physical containers may work: imagine reading an adventure book wrapped in a hammock or watching the movie *Jaws* in an underwater cinema!

6

ECONOMICS & POLITICS

Money allows
me to buy
what I want.

Ohne Geld
kann ich mir
nichts kaufen.

お金が無ければ
何も買えない。

MONEY IS
ENABLEMENT

You cannot eat money, but it can buy you food.

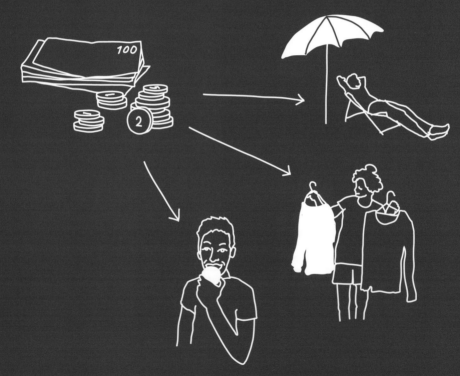

Research

People perceive money as something that allows them to experience or to buy things. Money as a physical object is often less valuable than the opportunities it stands for. When asked to define money, people of all ages highlight possibilities and opportunities.[127] In consequence, money is not about the physical coins or digital numbers, but the doors it can open and the things it can make possible.

Application

Thinking of money in terms of opportunities and possibilities allows for dealing with money in alternative ways. Imagine that, instead of displaying numbers in a bank account, the banking application showed affordable items from your personal wish list; the presents you could give to your spouse and children; or the number of people you could support in the developing world.

That wedding ring must cost a hefty sum.

Sein Vater hat ihm eine millionen-schwere Villa hingestellt.

中小企業は重い税に苦しんでいる。

CHEAP
IS LIGHT

EXPENSIVE
IS HEAVY

**Heavy objects
seem more precious
than lighter ones.**

Research

Imagine you are invited to a dinner party and want to buy a decent bottle of wine as a present. The supermarket you stepped into has a wide selection, but you are not sure which wine to choose and you closely inspect several options. Research suggests that you will not only consider the attributes of the wine, such as its country of origin, but also the weight of the bottle.[128] If you are looking for an expensive and high-quality present, you are more likely to select one of the heavier bottles.

Application

Restaurants or cafés that want to appear expensive and high-class employ heavier cutlery. The same concept works with books, jewellery, furniture, electronic devices and other products. Sometimes the products are heavier because they use more or denser material to support robustness and longevity; sometimes the additional weight is a just a selling device.

He is under
my power.

Alles unter
Kontrolle.

山田部長の下で
働いています。

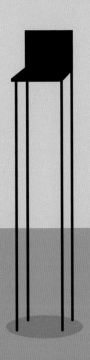

**SOCIAL
STATUS
IS UP**

**HAVING
NO SAY
IS DOWN**

235

People with high social status overestimate their own height.

Research

How people see the physical world seems to be influenced by their experience of social status and power. People with a higher social status underestimate the height of others[129] and overestimate their own height.[130] This also works the other way round: tall men are perceived as more charismatic leaders – suggesting one reason why tall individuals earn more money and end up higher on the career ladder.[131]

Application

Leaders are shown at the top of an organisation chart and voters are shown below parliamentarians in diagrams about the election system. Thus, if you are a supporter of flat hierarchies, make sure the charts show it!

He owes her a heavy debt.

Sie wird die Schulden die nächsten Jahr-zehnte mit sich rumschleppen.

過重な債務を抱えている。

DEBTS

ARE HEAVY

Want to lose weight? Lose debt!

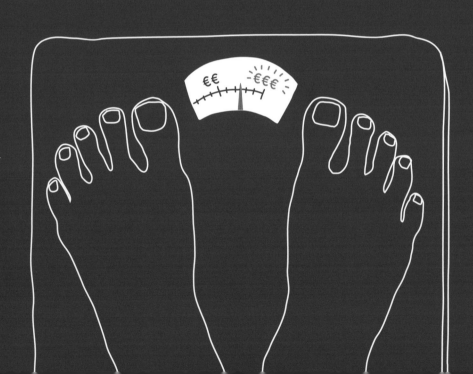

Research

Debts can constrain our freedom in daily choices like going out, having a vacation or buying birthday presents for the children. Owing money to others also impacts our psychological and bodily well-being: people in financial debt are more likely to suffer from depression[132] and they tend to gain physical weight.[133]

Application

Strategies supporting weight loss can go beyond focussing on food and exercise. Since financial circumstances influence mental health and obesity, any help with losing financial burdens might also help with losing physical weight.

Energy allows me to do my work with ease.

Das kann ich nur mit viel Energie schaffen.

それは元気が十分になければできない。

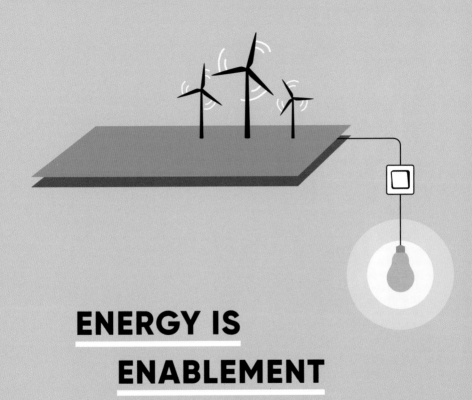

ENERGY IS
ENABLEMENT

**Energy is the ability
to make a difference.**

Research

When people of different cultures[134] and age groups[135] are asked to describe what *energy* means to them, their most common answer is that it enables them to do something. This holds true for different energy types, such as mechanical, electrical or mental energy.

Application

Enablement can be passive or active. While passive enablement just lets us do things without hindrance (e.g. opening a door that is unlocked), active enablement actively supports what we are doing (e.g. an exoskeleton). Many machines like robots, bicycles or computers are built to actively enable us, i.e. making us stronger, faster, more persistent and even smarter.

We made lots
of forward
movement.

Damit sind
wir gut voran-
gekommen.

この発見で
研究は大きく
前進した。

ACHIEVEMENT IS
FORWARD MOVEMENT
ON A PATH

Travelling the path
to success.

Research

Simple tasks can be solved faster when people see animations implying forward motion. In one study, participants who saw an animation that looked like they were moving forwards through a tunnel, solved word puzzles faster than those who did not see the animation.[136] People are also faster moving a joystick forwards when they read success words like *accomplish* or *achieve* than when they read failure words like *lose* and *flounder.*[137]

Application

The academic achievement of students can be promoted with images of forward movement on a path. When freshers complete worksheets depicting their college years as being on a path ahead, they are more interested in academic workshops and show greater stamina in solving maths problems. When students work on such sheets before their final exams, they plan more time for learning and less time for socialising, and even receive slightly better grades.[138]

The govern-
ment tried to
block an agree-
ment on farm
subsidies.

Die Partei steht
sich häufig
selbst im Weg.

反対派の
立ち入りを
阻止する。

IMPEDIMENTS TO ACTION
ARE BLOCKAGES

Accessible democracy.

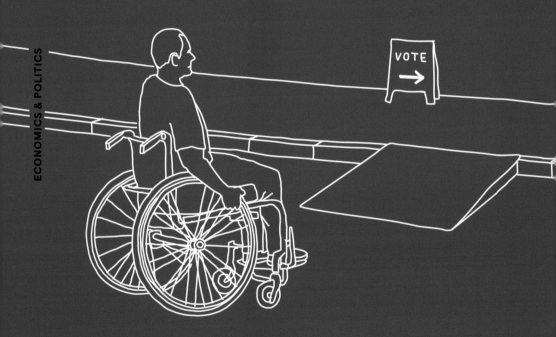

VOTE

→

Research

Physical disability often has social and psychological blocking effects. Citizens with disabilities are, for example, less likely to vote than their non-disabled counterparts. Best practices suggest removing physical obstacles by increasing physical polling-place accessibility and removing mental obstacles by education.[139]

Application

When we interact with computers, blockages can go many ways. When we block contacts in a messenger application, for example, the computer stops messages, calls and status updates coming through from these contacts. When we enter a wrong password, the computer blocks us with an error message. And *digital detox* means to block off our devices from interfering with our lives.

This politician represents a right-wing party.

Sie gehören zum linken Flügel der Partei.

右寄りの保守政党に投票する。

SOCIAL-DEMOCRATIC IS LEFT 〈 〉 **CONSER-VATIVE IS RIGHT**

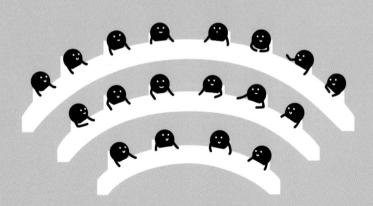

A dirty trick? Chairs can manipulate attitudes.

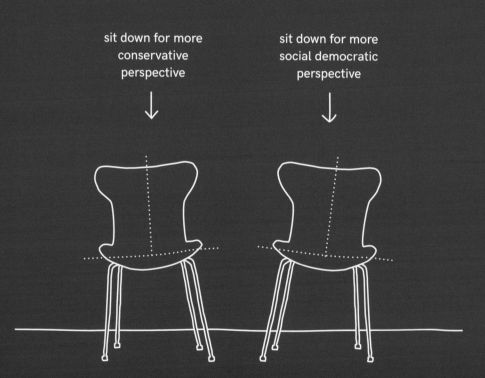

sit down for more
conservative
perspective

sit down for more
social democratic
perspective

Research

Our ideas about the political spectrum go back to the French Legislative Assembly in 1791, where conservative members sat on the right side of the president and liberal members on his left. This seating order became a metaphor for political orientation and is deeply embedded in our thinking and acting. Behavioural scientists found, for example, that people automatically order words with political meaning from left (liberal) to right (conservative) – even if not instructed to do so. In another study, participants listened to political words via headphones. They perceived conservative words as being louder in their right ear and liberal words as being louder in their left ear.[140]

Application

US citizens who are sitting in a chair tilting slightly to the left are more likely to agree with statements of the Democratic Party than those sitting in a chair tilting slightly to the right.[141] Thus, election observers should also monitor whether seats in polling booths are standing evenly!

7

ETHICS & TRANSCENDENCE

And Jesus said: "I am the Light of the World."

Ihr seid das Licht der Welt!

その仏像は神々しい光を放っている。

THE SACRED

IS BRIGHT

THE

PROFANE

IS DARK

Have you ever been blessed by a robot?

Research

In sacred art, faith, spirituality and holiness are often illustrated through light. Angels, for example, are often depicted with halos around their heads. Thus, it is not surprising that participants in an experiment matched brightly coloured objects to the word *religious* and darkly coloured objects to the word *godless*.[142]

Application

When spiritual services are offered by robots or smart speakers, these could enhance the user's experience by applying bright light. For example, the blessing robot *BlessU2* projects beams of light from its palms[143] and the coloured ring on the Amazon Echo speaker could light up like a halo when reciting religious texts.

No one involved in the conflict has clean hands.

Sie arbeiten mit schmutzigen Mitteln.

身の潔白を証明する。

**MORAL
IS CLEAN**

**IMMORAL
IS DIRTY**

Dirty hands?
Wash away your sins ...

Research

In a highly regarded study, participants lied to a colleague or told the truth, either by email or by voice message. Afterwards, they rated the desirability of several products. It turned out that hand sanitiser was particularly desirable after lying by email and mouthwash was particularly desirable after lying by voice mail.[144]

Application

Did your parents ever threaten to wash your mouth out with soap if you talked dirty? Have you ever wanted to clean your hands after an immoral act? This could be an opportunity for drug store ads. Do not wash, however, after doing something virtuous and the good feeling can prevail.

MORAL IS CLEAN – IMMORAL IS DIRTY

The future
looks bright.

Dieses Land
hat eine dunkle
Vergangenheit.

国民は明るい政治を
期待している。

GOOD

IS BRIGHT

EVIL IS DARK

269

Teams with dark shirts play more aggressively.

Research

In the 1980s, scientists found that sports teams wearing black clothes were more aggressive and received more penalties.[145] But darkness and moral behaviour also go together. People behave less morally when in a dark room or when wearing dark shades.[146] Similarly, writing about an unethical deed makes a room seem darker.[147]

Application

In the *Star Wars* series, the *Sith* are major practitioners of the dark side of *the Force* and they use *the Force* without moral restraint. They draw their powers from darker emotions like fear, anger, hatred and aggression. Giving expression to their moral values, they wear all black. The *Jedi* are practitioners of the light side of *the Force* and they are generally concerned with the ideas of good, generosity and healing. They meditate to clear themselves of negative emotion and only use their powers for knowledge and righteous defence. Accordingly, their clothing is kept in natural and brighter tones like brown and white.

I admire the
rectitude of
her character.

Er drehte
ein krummes
Ding.

彼は真っ直ぐな
性格で、嘘が
付けない。

MORAL IS STRAIGHT

Immoral characters are illustrated by a crooked appearance.

Research

In one study, participants were given abstract words, one at a time, and they said which of two metal rods, straight or bent, represented these words best. In each case, more than 80% of the participants followed the metaphor. They reached for the crooked rod to represent the concepts *incorrect, corrupt, illegal* and *dishonest*, and they reached for the straight rod to represent the concepts *correct, moral, legal* and *honest*.[148]

Application

The movie industry has long been using crookedness to characterise doubtful characters. In *The Lion King*, to emphasise the character Scar's immoral nature, he is presented with a bent neck and his mane appears crooked. In contrast, the moral character Mufasa walks around straight and his entire visual appearance is upright.

It's this one here that I want.

Das soll mir fernbleiben.

彼はどうも敬遠したい人物だ。

BAD IS FAR

GOOD IS

NEAR

Exercising to push away alcoholic drinks can help people get off the booze.

Research

In an experiment, participants responded to positive and negative words by either pulling or pushing a lever, thus moving the lever nearer to themselves or moving it further away. When a positive word like *friend* was shown, participants were much quicker to pull the lever towards themselves compared to when a negative word like *alcoholism* was shown.[149]

Application

Alcoholic patients can be trained to avoid alcoholic beverages by a similar exercise. Patients push a joy-stick each time they see pictures of alcoholic beverages and pull the joystick when they see non-alcoholic soft drinks. After just four sessions, the patients' approach bias for alcohol can change into an avoidance bias, and one year later these patients show better outcomes than patients without such training.[150]

She felt a heavy burden of guilt for her actions.

Er hat schwere Schuld auf sich geladen.

彼は重い罪を犯した。

GUILTY IS HEAVY

INNOCENT IS LIGHT

Forgiveness makes you feel lighter, perceive hills to be less steep and even jump higher!

Research

Unethical behaviour has a strong influence on our perception of weight. Participants in a study rated their own weight as higher when they had recalled unethical behaviour. Also, they perceived heavy physical tasks (e.g. carrying a basket of laundry for someone) as more demanding.[151]

Application

Sometimes people have unjustified guilty feelings. A simple act of forgiveness can help them to feel physically relieved. People who remember acts of forgiving perceive hills to be less steep and jump higher than people who remember unforgivingness.[152]

She was an
upright citizen.

Das waren
doch niedere
Beweggründe!

この犯罪集団は、
下劣なやり方で
悪銭を得ていた。

**MORAL
IS UP**

**IMMORAL
IS DOWN**

285

Does an upright posture cause more ethical behaviour?

Research

People recognise words with a positive moral meaning (e.g. *God*) faster when these are presented at the top of a screen compared to the bottom of the screen.[153] Moreover, researchers found that people shared more money with others when they were standing in an upright position than when sitting in a crouched position – but only in a context highlighting moral behaviour.[154]

Application

People rate strangers as being more religious or more moral when they are shown at the top of a computer screen.[155] So, if you want to be perceived as more virtuous than others, it might help to pay for your profile to be shown at the top!

She carries a heavy burden running the entire business alone.

Er nimmt das zu sehr auf die leichte Schulter.

彼の判断は
あまりに
軽率だった。

RESPONSIBLE
IS HEAVY

IRRESPONSIBLE
IS LIGHT

289

Are you able to carry the responsibility?

Research

People associate the concept of personal responsibility with physical weight. In one study, for example, participants took more responsible decisions when they were working on heavy clipboards compared to lighter ones. They differentiated better between strong and weak arguments and gave more consistent responses.[156]

Application

Inauguration ceremonies are often invoked when an office with great responsibilities is conferred to an individual. During a ceremony for a king, for example, he might receive a heavy crown and sceptre. In a traditional university, a newly elected president might receive a heavy necklace. Simply handing over a lightweight certificate of appointment just does not feel appropriate!

291

Curious who is behind the book?

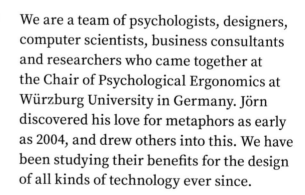

We are a team of psychologists, designers, computer scientists, business consultants and researchers who came together at the Chair of Psychological Ergonomics at Würzburg University in Germany. Jörn discovered his love for metaphors as early as 2004, and drew others into this. We have been studying their benefits for the design of all kinds of technology ever since.

Jörn Hurtienne

My aim is to make interactive technology intuitive to use and to provide meaningful user experiences. Metaphors can be mentally processed with little effort, making them interesting for design. At Würzburg University I hold the chair in Psychological Ergonomics. My favourite metaphor: **CONCRETE IS NEAR – ABSTRACT IS FAR.**

Diana Löffler

I am a postdoc researcher in human-computer interaction with a background in psychology. I love metaphors because they can be applied to all sorts of technology. Recently, I have taught metaphors to robots so they can interact with us more easily. My favourite metaphor: **ANGER IS HEAT.**

Clara Hüsch

Primary metaphors help to create good and brain-friendly designs. However, they also show how the human brain can be biased and manipulable. As a communication and information designer, I think it is essential to deal with metaphors consciously. My favourite metaphor: **LIFE IS A JOURNEY ON A PATH.**

Daniel Reinhardt

I am a computer scientist who specialises in human-computer interaction research. Primary metaphors open design spaces for embodied interaction and support us in creating novel interaction experiences. My favourite metaphor: **EXCITING IS ROUGH – BORING IS SMOOTH**.

Robert Tscharn

I am a management consultant and co-founder of the UX agency fuenfpunktnull. We craft the world and technology around us anyway, so why not directly align it with how humans think? My favourite metaphor: **MORAL IS UP – IMMORAL IS DOWN**.

Stephan Huber

I like how metaphors offer easy ways to understand our thinking. My first contact with primary metaphors was during my HCI Master's course. Since then, I have been looking into how people with few cognitive resources can be involved in design processes. My favourite metaphor: **ENERGY IS ENABLEMENT**.

You want more?

If you want to dig deeper into primary metaphors, we recommend the following sources.

More theory:
Lakoff & Johnson (1980)[157], Johnson (1987)[158], Grady (1997)[159]

More conceptual metaphors ... in linguistics:
Kövecses (2005, 2010)[160 161], Hampe (2017)[162], Littlemore (2019)[163]

... in philosophy:
Lakoff & Johnson (1999)[164]

... in social psychology:
Landau (2014, 2017)[165 166]

... in film:
Coegnarts (2015)[167], Fahlenbrach (2016)[168]

... in human-computer interaction and software design:
Hurtienne (2017)[169], Löffler et al. (2018)[170]

More examples of primary metaphors in linguistic expressions and in user interfaces of all sorts can be found in the research database ISCAT: iscat.psyergo.uni-wuerzburg.de

References

1   Lakoff, G., & Johnson, M. (1980). *Metaphors we live by.* Chicago: University of Chicago Press.

2   Steen, G. J., Dorst, A. G., Herrmann, J. B., Kaal, A., Krennmayr, T., & Pasma, T. (2010). *A method for linguistic metaphor identification: From MIP to MIPVU.* Amsterdam: John Benjamins.

3   Cienki, A. (1998). STRAIGHT: An image schema and its metaphorical extensions. *Cognitive Linguistics, 9*(2), 107–149.

4   Lakoff & Johnson (1980). See reference 1.

5   Grady, J. (1997). *Foundations of meaning: Primary metaphors and primary scenes* (Unpublished dissertation). Berkeley: University of California.

6   Löffler, D., Arlt, L., Toriizuka, T., Tscharn, R., & Hurtienne, J. (2016). Substituting color for haptic attributes in conceptual metaphors for tangible interaction design. In *Proceedings of the TEI'16: Tenth International Conference on Tangible, Embedded, and Embodied Interaction* (pp. 118–125). New York: ACM.

7   Williams, L. E., & Bargh, J. A. (2008). Experiencing physical warmth promotes interpersonal warmth. *Science, 322*(5901), 606–607.

8   Hurtienne, J. (2017). How cognitive linguistics inspires HCI: Image schemas and image-schematic metaphors. *International Journal of Human-Computer Interaction, 33*(1), 1–20.

9   Hurtienne, J. (2014). *Primary metaphors describe standard meanings of topological arrangements.* Paper presented at the Workshop Ubicomp beyond Devices: Objects, People, Space and Meaning at the 8th Nordic Conference on Human-Computer Interaction. Helsinki. Retrieved April 12, 2020, from http://www.meaningofspace.org/Papers_files/posm14_submission_7.pdf

10   Carney, D. R., Cuddy, A. J. C., & Yap, A. J. (2015). Review and summary of research on the embodied effects of expansive (vs. contractive) nonverbal displays. *Psychological Science, 26*(5), 657–663.

11   Ranehill, E., Dreber, A., Johannesson, M., Leiberg, S., Sul, S., & Weber, R. A. (2015). Assessing the robustness of power posing: No effect on hormones and risk tolerance in a large sample of men and women. *Psychological Science, 26*(5), 653–656.

12   Ackerman, J. M., Nocera, C. C., & Bargh, J. A. (2010). Incidental haptic sensations influence social judgments and decisions. *Science, 328*(5986), 1712–1715.

13   Hurtienne, J., Stößel, C., & Weber, K. (2009). Sad is heavy and happy is light: Population stereotypes of tangible object attributes. In *Proceedings of the TEI'09: Third International Conference on Tangible and Embedded Interaction* (pp. 61–68). New York: ACM.

14   Macaranas, A., Antle, A. N., & Riecke, B. E. (2012). Bridging the gap: Attribute and spatial metaphors for tangible interface design. In *Proceedings of the TEI'12: Sixth International Conference on Tangible, Embedded and Embodied Interaction* (pp. 161–168). New York: ACM.

15   Hurtienne, J., & Reinhardt, D. (2017). Texture metaphors and tangible interaction: No smooth relationship? In *Proceedings of TEI'17: Eleventh International Conference on Tangible, Embedded, and Embodied Interaction* (pp. 79–87). New York: ACM.

16 Hurtienne, J., Stößel, C., Sturm, C., Maus, A., Rötting, M., Langdon, P., & Clarkson, J. (2010). Physical gestures for abstract concepts: Inclusive design with primary metaphors. *Interacting with Computers, 22*(6), 475–484.

17 Ibid.

18 Casasanto, D., & Jasmin, K. (2012). The hands of time: Temporal gestures in English speakers. *Cognitive Linguistics, 23*(4), 643–674.

19 De la Fuente, J., Santiago, J., Román, A., Dumitrache, C., & Casasanto, D. (2014). When you think about it, your past is in front of you: How culture shapes spatial conceptions of time. *Psychological Science, 25*(9), 1682–1690.

20 Boroditsky, L. (2001). Does language shape thought?: Mandarin and English speakers' conceptions of time. *Cognitive Psychology, 43*(1), 1–22.

21 Hurtienne, J., & Meschke, O. (2016). Soft pillows and the near and dear: physical-to-abstract mappings with image-schematic metaphors. In *Proceedings of the TEI '16: Tenth International Conference on Tangible, Embedded, and Embodied Interaction* (pp.324–331). New York: ACM.

22 Mosher, M., & Tinapple, D. (2016). What We Have Lost / What We Have Gained: tangible interactions between physical and digital bodies. In *Proceedings of the TEI'16: Tenth International Conference on Tangible, Embedded, and Embodied Interaction* (pp. 658–662). New York: ACM.

23 Hurtienne et al. (2010). See reference 16.

24 Miles, L. K., Nind, L. K., & Macrae, C. N. (2010). Moving through time. *Psychological Science, 21*(2), 222–223.

25 Hazel, J. R. (1989). Cold adaptation in ectotherms: Regulation of membrane function and cellular metabolism. In L. C. H. Wang (Ed.), *Animal Adaptation to Cold* (pp. 1–50). Berlin, Heidelberg: Springer.

26 Löffler et al. (2016). See reference 6.

27 Taylor, C. (1930). Visual perception versus visual plus kinaesthetic perception in judging colored weights. *Journal of General Psychology, 4*(1–4), 229–246.

28 Buckingham, G., Cant, J. S., & Goodale, M. A. (2009). Living in a material world: how visual cues to material properties affect the way that we lift objects and perceive their weight. *Journal of Neurophysiology, 102*(6), 3111–3118.

29 Löffler, D. (2017). *Color, metaphor and culture – empirical foundations for user interface design* (Doctoral thesis, University of Würzburg, Germany). Retrieved April 12, 2020, from https://nbn-resolving.org/urn:nbn:de:b-vb:20-opus-153782.

30 Landau, M. J. (2018). Using metaphor to find meaning in life. *Review of General Psychology, 22*(1), 62–72.

31 Baldwin, M., Landau, M. J., & Swanson, T. J. (2018). Metaphors can give life meaning. *Self and Identity, 17*(2), 163–193.

32 Keefer, L. A., Landau, M. J., Sullivan, D., & Rothschild, Z. K. (2011). Exploring metaphor's epistemic function: Uncertainty moderates metaphor-consistent priming effects on social perceptions. *Journal of Experimental Social Psychology, 47*(3), 657–660.

33 Hurtienne, J., & Langdon, P. (2010). Keeping warm in winter: Image-schematic metaphors and their role in the design of central heating controls. In *Proceedings of the Fourth*

International Conference of the German Cognitive Linguistics Association (pp. 53–54). Bremen: University of Bremen, Germany.

34 Topolinski, S., & Sparenberg, P. (2012). Turning the hands of time: Clockwise movements increase preference for novelty. *Social Psychological and Personality Science, 3*(3), 308–314.

35 Löffler (2017). See reference 29.

36 Macaranas et al. (2012). See reference 14.

37 Hurtienne et al. (2009). See reference 13.

38 Krause, F., Bekkering, H., Pratt, J., & Lindemann, O. (2017). Interaction between numbers and size during visual search. *Psychological Research, 81*(3), 664–677.

39 SumBlox (2020). Math Blocks. Retrieved April 26, 2020, from https://sumblox.com

40 Meier, B. P., Robinson, M. D., & Caven, A. J. (2008). Why a Big Mac is a good Mac: Associations between affect and size. *Basic and Applied Social Psychology, 30*(1), 46–55.

41 Fong, D. K. C., Fong, L. H. N., Chark, R., & Chui, P. M. W. (2018). The bias of size in gambling decisions: Evidence from a casino game. *Cornell Hospitality Quarterly, 59*(1), 78–84.

42 Rolls, E. T. (2010). The affective and cognitive processing of touch, oral texture, and temperature in the brain. *Neuroscience & Biobehavioral Reviews, 34*(2), 237–245.

43 Stiehl, W. D., Breazeal, C., Han, K. H., Lieberman, J., Lalla, L., Maymin, A., ... & Kishore, A. (2006). The huggable: a therapeutic robotic companion for relational, affective touch. In *Proceedings of ACM SIGGRAPH'06 Conference on Emerging Technologies* (p. 15). New York: ACM.

44 Levinson, B. M. (1984). Human/companion animal therapy. *Journal of Contemporary Psychotherapy, 14*(2), 131–144.

45 Mannay, D. (2013). "I like rough pubs": Exploring places of safety and danger in violent and abusive relationships. *Families, Relationships and Societies, 2*(1), 131–137.

46 Macaranas et al. (2012). See reference 14.

47 Hurtienne et al. (2009). See reference 13.

48 Schneider, I. K., Parzuchowski, M., Wojciszke, B., Schwarz, N., & Koole, S. L. (2015). Weighty data: Importance information influences estimated weight of digital information storage devices. *Frontiers in Psychology, 5*(1536).

49 Anderson, Z., Jones, M., & Seppi, K. (2018). W.O.U.S.: Widgets Of Unusual Size. In *Proceedings of the TEI'18: Twelfth International Conference on Tangible, Embedded and Embodied Interaction* (pp. 221–230). New York: ACM.

50 Casasanto, D., & Jasmin, K. (2010). Good and bad in the hands of politicians: Spontaneous gestures during positive and negative speech. *PLOS ONE, 5*(7), Retrieved November 17, 2010, from http://www.plosone.org/article/info:doi/10.1371/journal.pone.0011805.

51 Casasanto, D. (2009). Embodiment of abstract concepts: good and bad in right- and left-handers. *Journal of Experimental Psychology: General, 138*(3), 351–367.

52 Kita, S., & Essegbey, J. (2001). Pointing left in Ghana: How a taboo on the use of the left hand influences gestural practice. *Gesture, 1*(1), 73–95.

53 Casasanto, D., Jasmin, K., Brookshire, G., & Gijssels, T. (2014). The QWERTY Effect: How typing shapes word meanings and baby

names. In P. Bello, M. Guarini, M. McShane, & B. Scassellati (Eds.), *Proceedings of the 36th Annual Conference of the Cognitive Science Society* (pp. 296–301). Austin, TX: Cognitive Science Society.

54 Winter, B., & Matlock, T. (2013). Making judgments based on similarity and proximity. *Metaphor and Symbol, 28*(4), 219–232.

55 Nekola, J. C., & White, P. S. (1999). The distance decay of similarity in bio-geography and ecology. *Journal of Biogeography, 26,* 867–878.

56 Hurtienne et al. (2010). See reference 16.

57 Löffler et al. (2016). See reference 6.

58 Ban, Y., Narumi, T., Fujii, T., Sakurai, S., Imura, J., Tanikawa, T., & Hirose, M. (2013). Augmented endurance: controlling fatigue while handling objects by affecting weight perception using augmented reality. In *Proceedings of the SIGCHI Conference on Human Factors in Computing Systems* (pp. 69–78). New York: ACM.

59 Meier, B. P., & Robinson, M. D. (2004). Why the sunny side is up: Associations between affect and vertical position. *Psychological Science, 15*(4), 243–247.

60 Crawford, L. E., Margolies, S. M., Drake, J. T., & Murphy, M. E. (2006). Affect biases memory of location: Evidence for the spatial representation of affect. *Cognition and Emotion 20*(8), 1153–1169.

61 Chandon, P., Hutchinson, J. W., Bradlow, E. T., & Young, S. H. (2009). Does In-Store Marketing Work? Effects of the Number and Position of Shelf Facings on Brand Attention and Evaluation at the Point of Purchase. *Journal of Marketing, 73*(6), 1–17.

62 Meier, B. P., Moller, A. C., Chen, J. J., & Riemer-Peltz, M. (2011). Spatial metaphor and real estate: North–South location biases housing preference. *Social Psychological and Personality Science, 2*(5), 547–553.

63 MacKay, K. J., & Fesenmaier, D. R. (1997). Pictorial element of destination in image formation. *Annals of Tourism Research, 24*(3), 537–565.

64 Marshall, D. (2002). The problem of the picturesque. *Eighteenth-Century Studies, 35*(3), 413–437.

65 Schneider et al. (2015). See reference 48.

66 Ackerman et al. (2010). See reference 12.

67 Jostmann, N. B., Lakens, D., & Schuber, T. W. (2009). Weight as an embodiment of importance. *Psychological Science 20*(9), 1169–1174.

68 Ackerman et al. (2010). See reference 12.

69 Savic, S., & Savicic, G. (2014). Unpleasant Design. Designing out unwanted behaviour. In *Proceedings of the 5th STS Italia Conference: A Matter of Design. Making Society through Science and Technology* (pp. 975–988). Milan: The Italian Society of Science and Technology Studies.

70 Hurtienne et al. (2009). See reference 13.

71 Löffler (2017). See reference 29.

72 Reece, A. G., & Danforth, C. M. (2017). Instagram photos reveal predictive markers of depression. *EPJ Data Science, 6*(1), 15.

73 Levitt, H., Korman, Y., & Angus, L. (2000). A metaphor analysis in treatments of depression: Metaphor as a marker of change. *Counselling Psychology Quarterly, 13*(1), 23–35.

74 Kleinsmith, A., De Silva, R., & Bianchi-Berthouze, N. (2006). Cross-cultural differences in recognizing affect from body posture. *Interacting with Computers 18*(6), 1371–1389.

75 Löffler, D., Schmidt, N., & Tscharn, R. (2018). Multimodal expression of artificial emotion in social robots using color, motion and sound. In *Proceedings of the HRI'18 International Conference on Human-Robot Interaction* (pp. 334–343). Chicaco: ACM.

76 Löffler et al. (2016). See reference 6.

77 Hurtienne et al. (2009). See reference 13.

78 Löffler (2017). See reference 29.

79 Schotte, D. E., Cools, J., & McNally, R. J. (1990). Film-induced negative affect triggers over-eating in restrained eaters. *Journal of Abnormal Psychology, 99*(3), 317.

80 Paykel, E. S. (1977). Depression and appetite. *Journal of Psychosomatic Research, 21*(5), 401–407.

81 Song, H., Vonasch, A. J., Meier, B. P., & Bargh, J. A. (2012). Brighten up: Smiles facilitate perceptual judgment of facial lightness. *Journal of Experimental Social Psychology, 48*(1), 450–452.

82 Dong, P., Huang, X., & Zhong, C. B. (2015). Ray of hope: Hopelessness increases preferences for brighter lighting. *Social Psychological and Personality Science, 6*(1), 84–91.

83 Löffler et al. (2018). See reference 75.

84 Muris, P., Merckelbach, H., Meesters, C., & Van Lier, P. (1997). What do children fear most often? *Journal of Behavior Therapy and Experimental Psychiatry, 28*(4), 263–267.

85 Fotios, S., Unwin, J., & Farrall, S. (2015). Road lighting and pedestrian reassurance after dark: A review. *Lighting Research & Technology, 47*(4), 449–469.

86 Rinck, M., & Becker, E. S. (2007). Approach and avoidance in fear of spiders. *Journal of Behavior Therapy and Experimental Psychiatry, 38*(2), 105–120.

87 Löffler et al. (2018). See reference 75.

88 Hurtienne et al. (2009). See reference 13.

89 Yu, N. (1995). Metaphorical expressions of anger and happiness in English and Chinese. *Metaphor and symbol, 10*(2), 59–92.

90 Chen, P. (2010). A cognitive study of "Anger" metaphors in English and Chinese idioms. *Asian Social Science, 6*(8), 73.

91 Löffler (2017). See reference 29.

92 Williams & Bargh (2008). See reference 7.

93 IJzerman, H., & Semin, G. R. (2009). The thermometer of social relations: Mapping social proximity on temperature. *Psychological Science, 20*(10), 1214–1220.

94 IJzerman, H., Gallucci, M., Pouw, W. T., Weißgerber, S. C., Van Doesum, N. J., & Williams, K. D. (2012). Cold-blooded loneliness: Social exclusion leads to lower skin temperatures. *Acta psychologica, 140*(3), 283–288.

95 Cramer, E. S., Matkin, B. B., & Antle, A. N. (2016). embodying alternate attitudes: Design opportunities for physical interfaces in persuasive gaming experiences. In *Proceedings of the TEI'16: Tenth International Conference on Tangible, Embedded, and Embodied Interaction* (pp. 404–409). New York: ACM.

96 Macaranas et al. (2012). See reference 14.

97   Williams, L. E., & Bargh, J. A. (2008). Keeping one's distance: The influence of spatial distance cues on affect and evaluation. *Psychological Science, 19*(3), 302–308.

98   Back, M. D., Schmukle, S. C., & Egloff, B. (2008). Becoming friends by chance. *Psychological Science, 19*(5), 439–440.

99   Cabibihan, J. J., & Chauhan, S. S. (2017). Physiological responses to affective tele-touch during induced emotional stimuli. *Transactions on Affective Computing 8*(1), 108–118.

100 Teh, J. K. S., Cheok, A. D., Choi, Y., Fernando, C. L., Peiris, R. L., & Fernando, O. N. N. (2009). Huggy Pajama: A parent and child hugging communication system. In *Proceedings of the 8th International Conference on Interaction Design and Children* (pp. 290–291). New York: ACM.

101 Samani, H. A., Parsani, R., Rodriguez, L. T., Saadatian, E., Dissanayake, K. H., & Cheok, A. D. (2012). Kissenger: Design of a kiss transmission device. In *Proceedings of the Designing Interactive Systems Conference* (pp. 48–57). New York: ACM.

102 Zeki, S. (2007). The neurobiology of love. *FEBS Letters, 581*(14), 2575–2579.

103 Lee, S. W., & Schwarz, N. (2014). Framing love: When it hurts to think we were made for each other. *Journal of Experimental Social Psychology, 54,* 61–67.

104 Gavelin, E. (2016). *Conceptual metaphors: a diachronic study of LOVE metaphors in Mariah Carey's song lyrics* (Student's thesis, Umea University, Sweden). Retrieved April 12, 2020 from http://www.diva-portal.org/smash/get/diva2:902296/FULLTEXT01.pdf

105 Gazit, S., Elkana, O., Dawidowicz, L., Yeshayahu, L., & Biran, I. (2017). Downwards vertical attention bias in conversion disorder vs controls: A pilot study. *Psychosomatics, 58*(6), 633–642.

106 Carney D. R., Cuddy A. J. C., & Yap A. J. (2010). Power posing: Brief nonverbal displays affect neuroendocrine levels and risk tolerance. *Psychological Science, 21*(10), 1363–1368.

107 Yap, A. J., Wazlawek, A. S., Lucas, B. J., Cuddy, A. J. C., & Carney, D. R. (2013). The ergonomics of dishonesty: the effect of incidental posture on stealing, cheating, and traffic violations. *Psychological Science, 24*(11), 2281–2289.

108 Hurtienne, J., Löffler, D., & Schmidt, J. (2014). Zur Ergonomie prosozialen Verhaltens: Kontextabhängige Einflüsse von Körperhaltungen auf die Ergebnisse in einem Diktatorspiel [Ergonomics of pro-social behavior: Context-dependent effects of postures on the results in a dictator game]. In A.C. Schütz, K. Drewing & K.R. Gegenfurter (Eds.) *Abstracts of the 56th Conference of Experimental Psychologists* (p. 117). Lengerich: Pabst.

109 Ackerman et al. (2010). See reference 12.

110 Antle, A. N., Corness, G., & Bevans, A. (2013). Balancing justice: Comparing whole body and controller-based interaction for an abstract domain. *International Journal of Arts and Technology, 6*(4), 388–409.

111 Anderson, C. A., Anderson, K. B., Dorr, N., DeNeve, K. M., & Flanagan, M. (2000). Temperature and aggression. *Advances in Experimental Social Psychology, 32,* 63–129.

112 Anderson, C. A. (2001). Heat and violence. *Current Directions in Psychological Science, 10,* 33–38.

113 Charteris-Black, J. (2004). *Corpus approaches to critical metaphor analysis.* Hampshire: Palgrave Macmillian.

114 Sullivan, K. (2015). Judging a book by its cover (and its background): effects of the metaphor intelligence is brightness on ratings of book images. *Visual Communication, 14*(1), 3–14.

115 Hurtienne (2014). See reference 9.

116 Wickens, C. D., & Carswell, C. M. (1995). The proximity compatibility principle: Its psychological foundation and relevance to display design. *Human Factors, 37*(3), 473–494.

117 Elsayed, M., Ismail, A. H., & Young, R. J. (1980). Intellectual differences of adult men related to age and physical fitness before and after an exercise program. *Journal of Gerontology, 35*(3), 383–387.

118 Fritz, N. E., McCarthy, C. J., & Adamo, D. E. (2017). Handgrip strength as a means of monitoring progression of cognitive decline: A scoping review. *Ageing Research Reviews, 35,* 112–123.

119 Jia, L., Hirt, E. R., & Karpen, S. C. (2009). Lessons from a Faraway land: The effect of spatial distance on creative cognition. *Journal of Experimental Social Psychology, 45*(5), 1127–1131.

120 Wakslak, C. (2010). *The effect of perspective on the evaluation of stock performance.* Unpublished manuscript, University of Southern California.

121 Van Horen, F., & Mussweiler, T. (2014). Soft assurance: Coping with uncertainty through haptic sensations. *Journal of Experimental Social Psychology, 54,* 73–80.

122 Forest, A. L., Kille, D. R., Wood, J. V., & Stehouwer, L. R. (2015). Turbulent times, rocky relationships: Relational consequences of experiencing physical instability. *Psychological Science, 26*(8), 1261–1271.

123 Miller, G. A. (1956). The magical number seven, plus or minus two: Some limits on our capacity for processing information. *Psychological review, 63*(2), 81.

124 Klingberg, T. (2009). *The overflowing brain: Information overload and the limits of working memory.* Oxford: Oxford University Press.

125 Hurtienne & Meschke (2016). See reference 21.

126 Bálint, K., & Tan, E. S. (2015). "It feels like there are hooks inside my chest": The construction of narrative absorption experiences using image schemata. *Projections, 9*(2), 63-88.

127 Tscharn, R. (2019). *Innovative and age-inclusive interaction design with image-schematic metaphors* (Doctoral thesis, University of Würzburg, Germany). Retrieved from https://nbn-resolving.org/urn:nbn:de:bvb:20-opus-175762

128 Piqueras-Fiszman, B., & Spence, C. (2012). The weight of the bottle as a possible extrinsic cue with which to estimate the price (and quality) of the wine? Observed correlations. *Food Quality and Preference, 25*(1), 41-45.

129 Yap, A. J., Mason, M. F., & Ames, D. R. (2013). The powerful size others down: The link between power and estimates of others' size. *Journal of Experimental Social Psychology, 49*(3), 591–594.

130 Duguid, M. M., & Goncalo, J. A. (2012). Living large: The powerful overestimate their own height. *Psychological Science, 23*(1), 36–40.

131 Hamstra, M. R. (2014). 'Big' men: Male leaders' height positively relates to followers' perception of charisma. *Personality and Individual Differences, 56,* 190–192.

132 Gathergood, J. (2012). Debt and depression: causal links and social norm effects. *The Economic Journal, 122*(563), 1094–1114.

133 Münster, E., & Letzel, S. (2008). Überschuldung, Gesundheit und soziale Netzwerke [Heavy indebtedness, health and social networks]. *Materialien zur Familienpolitik, 22,* 55–129.

134 Löffler, D., Lindner, K., & Hurtienne, J. (2014). Mixing languages: image-schema inspired designs for rural Africa. In *Proceedings of CHI'14 Extended Abstracts on Human Factors in Computing Systems* (pp. 1999–2004). New York: ACM.

135 Tscharn (2019). See reference 127.

136 Natanzon, M., & Ferguson, M. J. (2012). Goal pursuit is grounded: The link between forward movement and achievement. *Journal of Experimental Social Psychology, 48*(1), 379–382.

137 Robinson, M. D., & Fetterman, A. K. (2015). The embodiment of success and failure as forward versus backward movements. *PLOS ONE, 10*(2), e0117285.

138 Landau, M. J., Oyserman, D., Keefer, L. A., & Smith, G. C. (2014). The college journey and academic engagement: How metaphor use enhances identity-based motivation. *Journal of Personality and Social Psychology, 106*(5), 679–698.

139 Schur, L., Adya, M., & Ameri, M. (2015). Accessible democracy: reducing voting obstacles for people with disabilities. *Election Law Journal, 14*(1), 60–65.

140 Farias, A. R., Garrido, M. V., & Semin, G. R. (2013) Converging modalities ground abstract categories: The case of politics. *PLOS ONE 8*(4), e60971.

141 Oppenheimer, D. M., & Trail, T. E. (2010). Why leaning to the left makes you lean to the left: Effect of spatial orientation on political attitudes. *Social Cognition, 28*(5), 651–661.

142 Hurtienne et al. (2009). See reference 13.

143 Löffler, D., Hurtienne, J., & Nord, I. (2019). Blessing Robot BlessU2: A discursive design study to understand the implications of social robots in religious contexts. *International Journal of Social Robotics, 20,* 1–18.

144 Lee, S. W., & Schwarz, N. (2010). Dirty hands and dirty mouths: Embodiment of the moral-purity metaphor is specific to the motor modality involved in moral transgression. *Psychological Science, 21*(10), 1423–1425.

145 Frank, M. G., & Gilovich, T. (1988). The dark side of self- and social perception: Black uniforms and aggression in professional sports. *Journal of Personality and Social Psychology, 54*(1), 74–85.

146 Zhong, C. B., Bohns, V. K., & Gino, F. (2010). Good lamps are the best police: Darkness increases dishonesty and self-interested behavior. *Psychological Science, 21*(3), 311–314.

147 Banerjee, P., Chatterjee, P., & Sinha, J. (2012). Is it light or dark? Recalling moral behavior changes perception of brightness. *Psychological Science, 23*(4), 407–409.

148 Hurtienne & Meschke (2016). See reference 21.

149 Chen, M., & Bargh, J. A. (1999). Consequences of automatic evaluation: Immediate behavioral predispositions to approach or avoid the stimulus. *Personality and Social Psychology Bulletin, 25*(2), 215–224.

150 Wiers, R. W., Eberl, C., Rinck, M., Becker, E. S., & Lindenmeyer, J. (2011). Retraining automatic action tendencies changes alcoholic patients' approach bias for alcohol and improves treatment outcome. *Psychological Science, 22*(4), 490–497.

151 Day, M. V., & Bobocel, D. R. (2013). The weight of a guilty conscience: Subjective body weight as an embodiment of guilt. *PLOS ONE, 8*(7), e69546.

152 Zheng, X., Fehr, R., Tai, K., Narayanan, J., & Gelfand, M. J. (2015). The unburdening effects of forgiveness: Effects on slant perception and jumping height. *Social Psychological and Personality Science, 6*(4), 431–438.

153 Meier, B. P., Sellbom, M., & Wygant, D. (2007). Failing to take the moral high ground: Psychopathy and the vertical representation of morality. *Personality and Individual Differences, 43*(4), 757–767.

154 Hurtienne, et al. (2014). See reference 108.

155 Meier et al. (2007). See reference 153.

156 Jostmann et al. (2009). See reference 67.

157 Lakoff & Johnson (1980). See reference 1.

158 Johnson, M. (1987). *The body in the mind: The bodily basis of meaning, imagination, and reason.* Chicago: University of Chicago Press.

159 Grady (1997). See reference 5.

160 Kövecses, Z. (2005). *Metaphor in culture: Universality and variation.* Cambridge: Cambridge University Press.

161 Kövecses, Z. (2010). *Metaphor: A Practical Introduction.* New York: Oxford University Press.

162 Hampe, B. (2017, Ed.). *Metaphor: Embodied Cognition and Discourse.* Cambridge: Cambridge University Press.

163 Littlemore, J. (2019). *Metaphors in the mind: sources of variation in embodied metaphor.* New York: Cambridge University Press.

164 Lakoff, G., & Johnson, M. (1999). *Philosophy in the flesh: The embodied mind and its challenge to Western thought.* New York: Basic Books.

165 Landau, M., Robinson, M. D., & Meier, B. P. (2014). *The power of metaphor: Examining its influence on social life.* Washington: American Psychological Association.

166 Landau, N. (2017). *Conceptual metaphor in social psychology: The poetics of everyday life.* New York: Routledge.

167 Coëgnarts, M. (2015). *Embodied cognition and cinema: The sensory-motor grounding of abstract meaning in film* (Unpublished dissertation). Universiteit Antwerpen, Belgium.

168 Fahlenbrach, K. (2016). *Embodied metaphors in film, television, and video games. Cognitive approaches.* New York, London: Routledge.

169 Hurtienne (2017). See reference 8.

170 Löffler, D., Hess, A., Maier, A., & Schmitt, H. (2018). *Die IBIS-Methode: Handbuch zur Anwendung von Image Schemas und Metaphern im Designprozess [The IBIS method: Manual for the application of image schemas and metaphors in the design process].* Retrieved April 12, 2020, from https://www.researchgate.net/publication/324606333_Die_IBIS-Methode_-_Handbuch_zur_Anwendung_von_Image_Schemas_und_Metaphern_im_Designprozess

The whole book in one picture.

Metaphors connect the abstract with the physical. For the primary metaphors in this book, the chart shows the abstract concepts on the left and the physical concepts on the right. The connecting lines carry the page numbers. The connection between *good/bad* and *big/small*, for example, stands for the metaphor **GOOD IS BIG – BAD IS SMALL** on page 63.

Read the chart as a detailed table of contents. Many more connections are possible, which are not explored in this book. *Love,* for example, is not only *path* and *part/whole; love* is *heat* and *attraction*, too! What are your primary metaphors?